D1648351

The
Quotable
Conservative

The Quotable Conservative

The Wit, Wisdom, and Insight of Freedom's Most Passionate Advocates

Compiled by
BILL ADLER

A Birch Lane Press Book
Published by Carol Publishing Group

A Birch Lane Press Book
Published by Carol Publishing Group

Birch Lane Press is a registered trademark of Carol Communications, Inc.
Editorial Offices: 600 Madison Avenue, New York, N.Y. 10022
Sales and Distribution Offices: 120 Enterprise Avenue, Secaucus, N.J. 07094
In Canada: Canadian Manda Group, One Atlantic Avenue, Suite 105, Toronto, Ontario M6K 3E7
Queries regarding rights and permissions should be addressed to Carol Publishing Group, 600 Madison Avenue, New York, N.Y. 10022

Carol Publishing Group Books are available at special discounts for bulk purchases, sales promotion, fund-raising, or educational purposes. Special editions can be created to specifications. For details, contact: Special Sales Department, Carol Publishing Group, 120 Enterprise Avenue, Secaucus, N.J. 07094.

Manufactured in the United States of America
10 9 8 7 6 5 4 3 2 1

Library of Congress Cataloging-in-Publication Data

The quotable conservative : the wit, wisdom, and insight of freedom's most passionate advocates / compiled by Bill Adler.
    p.   cm.
    "A Birch Lane Press book."
    ISBN 1-55972-291-6
    1. Conservatism—Quotations, maxims, etc.   I. Adler, Bill.
JC573.Q67   1995
320.5′2—dc20   94-44942
                                                 CIP

Contents

Introduction

True power stems from the spoken word. History has aptly demonstrated that military might and missiles pale in comparison to the power of thought.

In *The Quotable Conservative* you will encounter some of the most powerful, most influential, most creative thoughts of our time. From the beginning of the conservative movement with Edmund Burke to contemporary days with Irving Kristol, Dan Quayle, and Newt Gingrich, conservative philosophy has proved to be a potent thought indeed.

From abortion to xenophobia, conservatives have a lot to say and a lot to offer. The conservative perspective tells us a lot about who we are, and about where we are going as a nation and society in the future. But you will find that not all conservatives agree on every issue. On drug policy and gays in the military there are considerable differences among bona fide conservatives. But this diversity of opinion adds greater strength to the conservative movement because it demonstrates creativity and fortitude.

In *The Quotable Conservative* you will find hours of entertainment, intellectual stimulation, a way to stump your friends, thought-provoking sayings, ideals to emulate, and ideas for political and social activism. Okay—so there's something here for your candidate's speech, too.

I think that you will enjoy reading *The Quotable Conservative* as much as I enjoyed compiling it.

Bill Adler
New York, New York

SOCIAL ISSUES

What Is Art?

It is bad enough that so much of what passes for art and entertainment these days is the rampant promiscuity and the casual cruelty of our popular culture. To ask us to pay for it is to add insult to injury. We will not be intimidated by our cultural guardians into accepting either the insult or the injury.

—FORMER SECRETARY OF EDUCATION WILLIAM BENNETT, *In an address to the Republican Convention,* August 19, 1992

As long as federal dollars are used to finance art projects, Congress will have the responsibility to its constituents to determine what type of art taxpayer dollars will support.

—PHILIP M. CRANE, U.S. CONGRESSMAN, *The New York Times,* May 21, 1990

Should federal funding of the arts be tied to content?

My answer: Of course. Congress has the clear responsibility to oversee the expenditure of all federal funds—including the arts.

The American people in the vast majority are aghast to learn that their tax money has been used to reward artists (e.g., the Mapplethorpe exhibit) who choose to depict sadomasochism, perverted homoerotic sex acts and even sexual exploitation of children.

—NORTH CAROLINA SENATOR JESSE HELMS, *USA Today,* September 8, 1989

Today to win the highest critical praise, or to receive leading Oscar consideration, you have to make a movie that says life is short and bitter, and it stinks.

—MOVIE CRITIC MICHAEL MEDVED, November 1992

Where there's liberty art succeeds. In societies that are not free, art dies.

—RONALD REAGAN, *The Washington Post,* August 1, 1990

Mark my words. It is only a matter of time before someone burns a flag, calls it "kinetic art" and gets a great grant to take his act on the road.

—JOURNALIST GEORGE WILL, *Wit and Wisdom of Politics,* 1992

The War on Drugs

You've got to exact some cost from the people who are sending these drugs into our country.

—SECRETARY OF EDUCATION WILLIAM J. BENNETT, *NBC, Meet the Press,*
March 19, 1989

Drugs are wrong. They burn out your brain and they sear your soul.

—WILLIAM J. BENNETT, *NBC, Meet the Press,* March 19, 1989

It's hard to fight the war when you've got to debate the worthiness of fighting it.

—WILLIAM J. BENNETT, *CNN, Evans & Novak,* December 16, 1989

It is widely assumed by the other side on the drug question that to decriminalize drugs would be to register a social assent to drug consumption. Several times in this space in years gone by the effort has been made to stress the contrary.

The initial problem is to make clear that to license an activity is not to approve it. We license the publication of Hustler magazine even as we gag at the knowledge of what goes on within its covers.

—EDITOR WILLIAM F. BUCKLEY JR., *The Buffalo News,* April 5, 1995

One is to prohibit the use of vending machines for cigarettes. And why not? It is already illegal in every state of the union to sell cigarettes to minors, but of course young people buy them anyway. Who is going to stop them? Who is going to notice? Beer can't be bought legally in most states until age 21, and it struck nobody as surprising that, under the circumstances, people can't just stuff coins into a machine and midwife a can of beer. Why should it be different with cigarettes?

—WILLIAM F. BUCKLEY JR., *The Record,* March 20, 1995

Drug dealers need to understand a simple fact. You shoot a cop and you're going to be severely punished—fast. And if I had my way, I'd say with your life.

—GEORGE BUSH, *The Washington Post,* March 10, 1989

The real drug "kingpin" is the user. It is the casual users who create the profits. But we can't put them all in prison; there isn't any room in the jails.

—TEXAS SENATOR PHIL GRAMM, *The New York Times,* September 11, 1988

I am opposed [to the legalization of marijuana]. And I am opposed because the score is not in yet [on the medical effects of its use]. The thing I think most people don't realize about legalization of marijuana is that fourteen companies have already registered trade names for marijuana cigarettes. Once you make them legal, you're going to see billboards, and packs in the vending machines. Since marijuana is smoked for effect—not for taste, as cigarettes—how are they going to advertise? What are they going to say—"Fly higher with ours"?

—RONALD REAGAN, *Sacramento, California,* June 22, 1972

The President [Carter] had ordered there be no hard liquor in the White House. And now we find some of the White House has been smoking pot. This is the first administration we can honestly say is high and dry.

—RONALD REAGAN, *Topeka, Kansas,* October 29, 1980

We're not really going to get anywhere until we take the criminality out of drugs.

—SECRETARY OF STATE GEORGE P. SCHULTZ, *PBS, McNeil-Lehrer News Hour,* December 18, 1989

We're frying the brains of children.

> —**WYOMING SENATOR ALAN K. SIMPSON,** *CNN, Evans & Novak,*
> September 17, 1989

If we want to lose the war on drugs, just leave it to law enforcement.

> —**U.S. ATTORNEY GENERAL RICHARD THORNBURGH,** *ABC, This Week With David Brinkley,* March 19, 1989

The Environment

For decades there has been a recurrent theme in radical environmentalism. Every problem is a "crisis," and every crisis demands immediate governmental action. In truth, the one consistent thread running through every perceived threat is that the more each is examined, the less there is to fear.

> —**BARRY ASMUS,** *author of "The Space Place", Imprimis,* January, 1992

No poor country does a good job protecting its environment.

> —**TEXAS SENATOR PHIL GRAMM,** *The Christian Science Monitor,*
> November 12, 1993

Besides the earth, man's principal resource is man himself.

> —**POPE JOHN PAUL II,** *Centesimus Annus,* 1991

And from the ancient forests of Oregon, to the Inland Empire of California, America's great middle class has got to start standing up to the environmental extremists who put insects, rats and birds ahead of families, workers and jobs.

—PATRICK BUCHANAN, *Presidential Candidate and Talk Show Commentator, in an address to the Republican Convention,* August 17, 1992

Fleas are a part of the ecological cycle, but I doubt if a dog thinks he is doing something to destroy ecology by wearing a flea collar.

—RONALD REAGAN, March 7, 1973

Heaven help us if government ever gets into the business of protecting us from ourselves.

—RONALD REAGAN, April 12, 1973

And on environmental issues he [her friend and Treasury official, Nick Ridley] was incomparably rational. He would not adopt a burdensome regulation or make an expensive commitment of public money simply because a newspaper or a pressure group had asserted that it was the "green" thing to do.

He always asked such questions as: What benefits will it bring? How much will it cost? How solid is the scientific evidence underlying this claim?

—MARGARET THATCHER, *commenting in Times Newspapers Limited,*
March 7, 1993

The Sanctity of Human Life

Public discussion of the decision almost completely ignores the Constitution and focuses instead on abortion. The inescapable fact is that the Constitution contains not one word that can be tortured into the slightest relevance to abortion, one way or the other. That is a subject left, like most subjects, to democratic processes. The court offered no legal reasoning for taking the abortion issue from the people by making abortion a constitutional right.

—SUPREME COURT NOMINEE ROBERT H. BORK, 1990

Faith, family—these are the values that sustain the greatest nation on Earth. And to these values we must add the infinitely precious value of life itself. Let me be clear: I support the right to life.

—GEORGE BUSH, March 3, 1992

Will America yield to the cold, inhospitable, unwelcoming jurisprudence of Roe vs. Wade? Or will we recover our founding traditions of hospitality to the stranger and the weak? The pro-abortion forces have given their answer. Happily, the American people have also given theirs—and it is a very different answer indeed.

—ILLINOIS REPRESENTATIVE HENRY HYDE, *Los Angeles Times,* July 23, 1989

Abortion is the killing of an innocently inconvenient human life.

—HENRY HYDE, *U.S. News & World Report,* May 4, 1981

Abortion is not a "lifestyle" issue. Abortion is not an issue for women only. Abortion is not an issue of the government's role in America's bedrooms.

The question of abortion—the task of securing the right of life of the unborn—is the most urgent civil rights issue of the 1990s. It depends on resolving anew the same question we answered regarding slavery—what value will our society assign to a human life?

—HENRY HYDE, *Roll Call,* September 28, 1992

We don't believe children are just mouths to feed. They are hearts, minds, and souls for our future. And they deserve our protection not only after their birth, but before they are born.

—NEW YORK REPRESENTATIVE JACK KEMP, *addressing the 1992 Republican Convention*

The advance of scientific evidence in recent years has favored the right to life. There is now no scientific doubt that what is aborted is not "part of a woman's body." It has, rather, an autonomous genctic code of its own. None of this is a matter of faith or theology.

Our whole people must now decide whether to grant this new individual human inclusive standing among Americans entitled to the constitutional protection of its government. Our people must declare who exactly we will count as "one among us," or expel from our protection.

—MICHAEL NOVAK, *Political Commentator and co-host of Evans & Novak, The St. Petersburg Times,* November 22, 1989

I've noticed that everybody that is for abortion has already been born.

—RONALD REAGAN, *The New York Times,* 1980

Our purpose is not to legislate family values. It is to ensure that Washington values families.

—RALPH REED JR., *Executive Director of the Christian Coalition, called for halting federal funding to Planned Parenthood and other organizations that perform abortions or abortion counseling in the United States or in foreign aid programs. The Charleston Gazette,* May 18, 1995

There is simply no credible foundation for the proposition that abortion is a fundamental right.

—KENNETH STARR, *U.S. Solicitor General, The New York Times,* November 24, 1989

Society and Race

Discrimination on the basis of race is illegal, immoral, and unconstitutional, inherently wrong, and destructive of democratic society.

—WILLIAM J. BENNETT, *Counting by Race (with Terry Eastland)*, 1979

If racial discrimination is to be tolerated whenever the government has some purpose in mind, however trivial the purpose and however attenuated the connection between the purpose and the discrimination, the courts will be in for some very ugly tasks. Federal and state regulators, and ultimately federal courts, will be called upon to determine the race of applicants for benefits. Indeed, they may be called upon to decide whether Congress may "benignly discriminate" in favor of blacks and Hispanics but not in favor of Arabs or, indeed, any of the many other ethnic minorities with which America abounds. In broadcasting, these groups would be quite as likely to create programming diversity as currently favored groups. Why, then, do they not have an equal-protection claim to the same preferences? No good answer exists.

—SUPREME COURT NOMINEE ROBERT H. BORK, *National Review*, December 31, 1990

Quotas don't help anyone. In fact, they are one of the worst forms of racial and gender-based discrimination. Every American citizen should be treated equally and should have equal opportunity under the law.

—NEW YORK SENATOR ALFONSE D'AMATO, *in a letter to the Editor, Newsday,* November 2, 1990

It is tempting to believe that social evils from arise the activities of evil men and that if only good men (like ourselves, naturally) wielded power, all would be well. That view requires only emotion and self-praise. To understand why it is that "good" men in positions of power will produce evil, while the ordinary man without power but able to engage in voluntary cooperation with his neighbors will produce good, requires analysis and thought, subordinating the emotions to the rational faculty.

—ECONOMIST MILTON FRIEDMAN, *The International Herald Tribune,* August 15, 1994

As President Reagan said, we are more concerned with your destination than your origin. But the Democrats want to force individuals into groups, establish quotas, and limit your future based on your genetic past.

—GEORGIA REPRESENTATIVE NEWT GINGRICH, *addressing the Republican Convention,* 1992

13

Job discrimination excludes qualified individuals, lowers work-force productivity and eventually hurts us all. Topping the new world order means attracting the best and creating a workplace environment where everyone can excel. Anything less makes us a second-rate nation. It's not just bad—it's bad business.

—FORMER SENATOR AND PRESIDENTIAL CANDIDATE BARRY GOLDWATER, *News Tribune,* July 18, 1994

All the '91 act did was clarify some things that were clearly up to the legislature. Our lasting achievements include the fact that preferences based on race have been widely questioned and that, at least in my perception, discrimination on the basis of race, in all respects, is down.

—FORMER U.S. ATTORNEY GENERAL ED MEESE 3RD, *commenting on the Civil Rights Act of 1991, The Connecticut Law Tribune,* January 11, 1993

The whole notion that you can equalize opportunity in the things that matter is utopian.

—COLUMNIST THOMAS SOWELL, *Senior Fellow, Hoover Institution,* 1992

Race should not be a source of power or advantage or disadvantage for anyone in a free society. This was one of the most important lessons of the original civil rights movement.

—ESSAYIST SHELBY STEELE, 1992

Black students have the lowest grade point average of any student group. If whites were not so preoccupied with escaping their own guilt, they would see that the real problem is not racism; it is that black students are failing in tragic numbers. They don't need separate dorms and yearbooks. They need basic academic skills. But instead they are taught that extra entitlements are their due and that the greatest power of all is the power that comes to them as victims. If they want to get anywhere in American life, they had better wear their victimization on their sleeve, they had better tap into white guilt, making whites want to escape by offering money, status, racial preferences—something, anything—in return. Is this the way for a race that has been oppressed to come into its own? Is this the way to achieve independence?

—SHELBY STEELE, 1992

Much has been said about blacks and conservation. Those on the left smugly assume blacks are monolithic and will by force of circumstances always huddle to the left of the political spectrum.

The political right watches this herd mentality in action, concedes that blacks are monolithic, picks up a few dissidents, and wistfully shrugs at the seemingly unbreakable hold the liberal left has on black Americans.

—SUPREME COURT NOMINEE CLARENCE THOMAS, *The San Francisco Chronicle,*
July 10, 1991

I am of the view that black Americans will move inexorably and naturally toward conservatism when we stop discouraging them; when they are treated as a diverse group with differing interests; and when conservatives stand up for what they believe in rather than against blacks. This is not a prescription for success, but rather an assertion that black Americans know what they want, and it is not timidity and condescension. Nor do I believe gadget ideas such as enterprise zones are of any consequence when blacks who live in blighted areas know that crime, not lack of tax credits, is the problem. Blacks are not stupid. And no matter how good an idea or proposal is, no one is going to give up the comfort of the leftist status quo as long as they view conservatives as antagonistic to their interests, and conservatives do little or nothing to dispel the perception.

—CLARENCE THOMAS, *Policy Review,* October 1991

Welfare and the Welfare State

New York is listed as the second most expensive city in the United States to live in, a mere one point under San Francisco. Rudimentary common sense argues against attracting chronic welfare mothers and children to a city in which life is tough, crime high, dope especially tempting, as it is for those who seek escapism. It is surely Mayor Giuliani's point a) that welfare can't be unlimited, and b) that no compassionate purposes are served in attracting the indigent to a city where unemployment is higher than the national average and the cost of living as unattractive as the winter weather.

—EDITOR WILLIAM F. BUCKLEY JR., *National Review*, June 12, 1995

And having looked to Government for bread, on the very first scarcity they will turn and bite the hand that fed them.

—BRITISH STATESMAN EDMUND BURKE, *Thoughts and Details on Scarcity*, 1800

Why be thrifty any longer when your old age and health care are provided for, no matter how profligate you may be in your youth? Why be prudent when the state insures your bank deposits, replaces your flooded-out house, buys all the wheat you can

We have 6000 years of written historical experience in the Judeo-Christian tradition. We know the rules that work. We know that learning, study, working, saving, and commitment are vital. That is why Republicans would replace welfare with work.

—GEORGIA REPRESENTATIVE NEWT GINGRICH,
addressing the 1992 Republican Convention

grow? Why be diligent when half your earnings are taken from you and given to the idle?

—DAVID FRUM, *Dead Right,* 1994

The welfare culture tells the man he is not a necessary part of the family; he feels dispensable, his wife knows he is dispensable, his children sense it.

—ECONOMIST AND AUTHOR GEORGE GILDER, *Wealth and Poverty,* 1980

The first priority of any serious program against poverty is to strengthen the male role in poor families.

—GEORGE GILDER, *Wealth and Poverty,* 1980

They are a disaster. They ruined the poor. They created a culture of poverty and a culture of violence which is destructive of this civilization, and they have to be replaced thoroughly from the ground up.

—NEWT GINGRICH, *commenting on Great Society programs, I, Newt: The Quotations of Speaker Gingrich,* 1994

In 1994, the top one percent of income-earners paid 26 percent of the total federal individual income taxes while making 13 percent of the pre-tax income. The top 10 percent paid 58 percent of taxes. The top 20 percent paid 73 percent of the taxes.

These are astounding figures, but they're accurate: They come from the latest edition of the "Overview of the Federal Tax System," published by the House Ways and Means Committee when the Democrats were still in the majority.

The poor, the lower-middle class and even the middle-middle class pay only a tiny proportion of federal income taxes. The bottom 40 percent of income-earners pay less than one percent. The bottom 60 percent pay only 10 percent. (These figures exclude Social Security taxes, which are supposed to be contributions toward retirement and health insurance.)

—JAMES K. GLASSMAN, *The Washington Post,* July 11, 1995

The American people endorse this basic approach: They want to fix what's broken, but they don't want to destroy the system and rebuild it in the image of the Post Office. That's where they disagree with the Clinton Administration and its Congressional allies. That is the great lesson of the current health care debate.

—TEXAS SENATOR PHIL GRAMM, *Roll Call,* September 26, 1994

Mandates kill jobs, but even worse, they cost Americans freedom.

—PHIL GRAMM, *USA Today,* May 18, 1994

To help them see through the double-speak of an earlier era, Winston Churchill laid out a series of simple questions that people could ask to determine if they lived in a free country. Let me propose three questions to help determine if the Clinton [health care] plan is built on true consumer choice:

If I'm happy with the private health insurance I now have, can I keep it?

If I become unhappy with the health care provided through the government-controlled plan, could I take my money out of that plan and put it into a private insurance plan?

Even if the government keeps my health-care money, can I pay twice for coverage—once for the government plan I don't want and a second time for the private health insurance I do want?

The answer to all three questions is "no." Once the American people understand that, the Clinton plan is doomed.

—PHIL GRAMM, *The Houston Chronicle,* February 17, 1994

We don't believe compassion should be measured by the size of the safety net, but by the number of rungs on the ladder of opportunity.

—NEW YORK REPRESENTATIVE JACK KEMP, *addressing the 1992 Republican Convention*

For 50 years, the Democratic Party has dictated most of the policies governing our cities. Higher taxes. Redistribution of wealth. A welfare system that penalizes people for working, discourages marriage, punishes the family, and literally prohibits savings. It's not the values of the poor that are flawed; it's the values of the welfare system that are bankrupt.

—JACK KEMP, *addressing the 1992 Republican Convention*

I am for lifting everyone off the social bottom. In fact, I am for doing away with the social bottom altogether.

—AUTHOR AND SOCIALITE CLARE BOOTH LUCE, *Time,* February 14, 1964

Incentives to fail.

—SOCIOLOGIST CHARLES MURRAY, *describing the welfare system, Policy Review,* Fall 1993

We tried to provide more for the poor and produced more poor instead. We tried to remove the barriers to escape poverty, and inadvertently built a trap.

—CHARLES MURRAY, *Losing Ground,* 1984

If we take the route of the permanent handout, the American character will itself be impoverished.

—RICHARD M. NIXON, August 8, 1969

There's no greater social program than a job, an opportunity.

—**DAN QUAYLE,** *David Frost Show,* September 24, 1992

Welfare's purpose should be to eliminate, as far as possible, the need for its own existence.

—**CALIFORNIA GOVERNOR RONALD REAGAN,** *Los Angeles Times,*
January 7, 1970

You know, I think the best possible social program is a job.

—**PRESIDENTIAL CANDIDATE RONALD REAGAN,** *Trevose, Pennsylvania,* 1980

Welfare dependency is stark evidence of the economic inviability of single motherhood. Because children learn what they live, intergenerational poverty is common. This should come as no surprise. The habits that welfare subsidizes and fosters are the same habits that, when inculcated in children, make it difficult to break loose from dependency.

—**RALPH REED JR., EXECUTIVE DIRECTOR OF THE CHRISTIAN COALITION,**
Policy Review, Summer 1993

Just as the tax code penalizes marriage and children, so does the welfare system subsidize family breakup.

—**RALPH REED JR.,** *Policy Review,* Summer 1993

Women

Somewhere out in this audience may even be someone who will one day follow in my footsteps and preside over the White House as the President's spouse. I wish him well.

—BARBARA BUSH, *Wellesley College,* 1990

The differences between the sexes are the single most important fact of human society.

—ECONOMIST AND AUTHOR GEORGE GILDER, *Men and Marriage,* 1992

I prefer to call the most obnoxious feminists what they really are: feminazis.

—RADIO TALK-SHOW HOST RUSH LIMBAUGH, *The Way Things Ought to Be,* 1992

Political liberals hold no monopoly on respecting women's abilities.

—MARILYN QUAYLE, *addressing the 1992 Republican Convention*

Maybe the trouble with those professional women's libbers I mentioned earlier is related to something Will Rogers once said,

"If women go on trying to be more and more equal to men, some day they won't know any more than men do."

—RONALD REAGAN, 1976

Supporting the Equal Rights Amendment is like trying to kill a fly with a sledge hammer. You don't kill the fly, but you end up breaking the furniture. . . .We cannot reduce women to equality. Equality is a step down for most women.

—PHYLLIS SCHLAFLY, *Author and Anti-Equal Rights Amendment Organizer,* *Boston Globe,* June 16, 1974

In politics if you want anything said, ask a man. If you want anything done, ask a woman.

—MARGARET THATCHER, *British Conservative Party Leader, People,* September 15, 1975

I've got a woman's ability to stick to a job and get on with it when everyone else walks off and leaves it.

—MARGARET THATCHER, 1975

AMERICA

America Is a Bouquet

The spirit of national machoism prevails, encouraged by an effete corps of impudent snobs who characterize themselves as intellectuals.

—SPIRO AGNEW, *New York Times,* October 20, 1969

The business of America is business.

—CALVIN COOLIDGE, January 17, 1923.

Those who argued for counterculture values, bigger government . . . and bureaucracies deciding how you should spend your money were on the losing end in virtually every part of the country.

—REPRESENTATIVE NEWT GINGRICH, *I, Newt: The Quotations of Speaker Gingrich,* 1994

Mothers' dreams do not die easily in America.

—SENATOR PHIL GRAMM, *addressing the 1992 Republican Convention*

What is our vision? Our vision for America is an America that is strong because ordinary people are given extraordinary opportunities. I do not believe that America is a great and powerful country because the most brilliant and talented people in the world came to live here. I am always trying to remind my children that they ought to thank God to live in America, because given the kind of people we are, we would be peasants in any other country on the planet. America is a great and powerful country because it was here that ordinary people like you and me had more opportunities and more freedom than any other people who have ever lived in history. With that opportunity and that freedom, ordinary people like us have been able to do extraordinary things. We want to make it possible for more ordinary Americans to do more extraordinary things. And we believe the path to that achievement is in limiting the power of government, by limiting the cost of government and by elevating the individual citizen and by reaffirming that individual's sovereignty. That's what the Republican cause is all about, and that's what this battle is about.

—PHIL GRAMM, February 18, 1993

We don't believe in an America that pursues equality by making rich people poor, but by allowing poor people, indeed all people, to become rich. Not just rich in creature comforts, but rich in the opportunity to achieve your God-given potential.

—**JACK KEMP,** addressing the 1992 Republican Convention

Americans never quit.

—**GENERAL DOUGLAS MACARTHUR,** *President of the American Olympic Committee, commenting when the manager of the American boxing team in the 1928 Olympic games wanted to withdraw the team because of what he thought was an unfair decision against an American boxer, The New York Times,* August 9, 1928

Those of us who shout the loudest about Americanism in making character assassinations are all too frequently those who, by our own words and acts, ignore some of the basic principles of Americanism—
The right to criticize.
The right to hold unpopular beliefs.
The right to protest.
The right of independent thought.

—**MAINE SENATOR MARGARET CHASE SMITH,** June 1, 1950

It is time to start looking out for the forgotten Americans right here in the United States.

—**PATRICK BUCHANAN,** *Time,* March 16, 1992

Democracy: A Fragile Flower

Many forms of government have been tried, and will be tried in this world of sin and woe. No one pretends that democracy is perfect or all-wise. Indeed, it has been said that democracy is the worst form of government except all those other forms that have been tried from time to time.

—**FORMER BRITISH PRIME MINISTER WINSTON CHURCHILL,** *in an address to the House of Commons,* 1947

If all that Americans want is security they can go to prison. They'll have enough to eat, a bed and a roof over their heads. But if an American wants to preserve his dignity and his equality as a human being, he must not bow his neck to any dictatorial government.

—**DWIGHT D. EISENHOWER,** 1949

Without exhaustive debate, even heated debate, of ideas and programs, free government would weaken and wither. But if we allow ourselves to be persuaded that every individual or party that takes issue with our own convictions is necessarily wicked or treasonous, then, indeed, we are approaching the end of freedom's road.

—**Dwight D. Eisenhower,** 1954

If there is one civil right more precious than all the rest, it is the right to vote.

—**Columnist James Kilpatrick,** *The Atlanta Journal and Constitution,* May 6, 1991

The only political system that seems to allow this inherent liberty to express itself in time and space is democracy. It is not enough to have spiritual liberty; people must be free to express themselves publicly in worldly structures and systems. Among such systems, democracy is assuredly flawed, like all things human. Yet no other system protects human rights as well. Democracy means not majority rule alone, but also the protection of human rights, including the rights of the unborn.

—**Michael Novak,** *Political commentator and Co-host of Evans & Novak, The Los Angeles Times,* December 24, 1989

All the world will learn in the Nineties that neither democracy nor enterprise is merely a bumper sticker slogan. Both entail an ethos, an ethic, a deeper interior and moral life than most of us have spent much time cultivating in ourselves in recent years.

—MICHAEL NOVAK, *Forbes,* November 27, 1989

What has happened to the dreams of the United Nation's founders? What has happened to the spirit which created the United Nations? The answer is clear: Government got in the way of the dreams of the people.

—RONALD REAGAN, *addressing the United Nations General Assembly,* September 26, 1983

We have the means to change the laws we find unjust or onerous. We cannot, as citizens, pick and choose the laws we will or will not obey.

—RONALD REAGAN, *explaining his dismissal of 12,000 striking air traffic controllers, Chicago,* September 3, 1981

The other day, someone told me the difference between a democracy and a people's democracy. It's the same difference between a jacket and a straightjacket.

—RONALD REAGAN, December 10, 1986

Democracy is not a fragile flower; it still needs cultivating.

—**RONALD REAGAN,** *addressing the British Parliament,* June 8, 1982

Voters don't decide issues, they decide who will decide issues.

—**JOURNALIST GEORGE WILL,** *Newsweek,* March 8, 1976

This was a victory for the American people. While the election is over, the work has just begun. We literally are going to need all your help. I can't say this too strongly. For America to succeed in the 20th century, Americans will have to succeed.

—**REPRESENTATIVE NEWT GINGRICH,** *seeking support from students and business leaders for his conservative agenda after the 1994 elections, The Atlanta Journal and Constitution,* November 18, 1994

Some folks still don't get it. The federal government's one-size-fits-all policy was repudiated by the voters in November, but true believers continue to look to Washington to solve our welfare problem while ignoring the extraordinarily creative reforms launched by states.

—**SENATOR PHIL GRAMM,** *USA Today,* February 1, 1995

Patriotism

If a multitude of individuals are also to be a community, they must have symbols by which they live, symbols that express their identity as a community. The United States is a large and increasingly diverse and pluralistic society. The one symbol that expresses our existence as a community, the one symbol that stands above all others as an expression of our nationhood, is the American flag. The flag should be preserved inviolate as the one symbol that stands above political and partisan ideological dispute.

—ROBERT H. BORK, *testifying before the House Judiciary Committee's subcommittee on civil and constitutional rights, supporting a Constitutional amendment prohibiting the desecration of the American flag,* August, 1989

The Bill of Rights is like the Ten Commandments, a syllabus of constraints: Thou shalt not legislate against free speech. And a flag-burning amendment can be viewed as a contradiction of one of these constraints: Thou shalt not interpret the First Amendment as authorizing the burning of the flag.

—EDITOR WILLIAM F. BUCKLEY JR., *The Buffalo News,* June 15, 1995

If limits deemed reasonable by reasonable citizens are placed on speech, are we so certain that we will have drowned out somebody who was about to give birth to the Areopagitica, or to the electric light bulb, or to the Rhapsody in Blue? It is easy to come up with the names of brave thinkers who think their thoughts when tyranny is in the saddle—Solzhenitsyn wrote while Khrushchev reigned. But how many geniuses would be stultified if laws were enacted against the advocacy of violence? We do not need such laws in America, A.D. 1995, but such laws were certainly needed in Peru. Has the suppression of the Shining Path deprived civilization of a great social or scientific insight?

—WILLIAM F. BUCKLEY JR., *National Review,* May 29, 1995

So to be patriots as not to forget we are gentlemen.

—BRITISH STATESMAN EDMUND BURKE, *Thoughts on the Cause of the Present Discontents,* April 23, 1770

The genius of America is our capacity for rebirth and renewal. America is the land where the sun is always peeking over the horizon.

—GEORGE BUSH, *from his acceptance speech as the Republican party's presidential candidate,* August 20, 1992

And I believe that America will always have a special place in God's heart, as long as he has a special place in ours. And maybe that's why I've always believed that patriotism is not just another point of view.

—GEORGE BUSH, August 20, 1992

The power of America rests in a stirring but simple idea—that people will do great things if only you set them free.

—GEORGE BUSH, *1992 State of the Union Address*

At work here is something larger than the flag itself: It is a protest against the vulgarization, the trashing of our society. This amendment [to prohibit flag burning] asserts that our flag is not just a piece of cloth, but, like a family picture on your desk, it represents certain unifying ideals most Americans hold sacred. It represents the "unum" in the "e pluribus unum" of our country, and as tombstones are not for toppling, as churches and synagogues and places of worship are not for vandalizing, flags are not for burning.

—REPRESENTATIVE HENRY HYDE, *The Christian Science Monitor,* July 5, 1995

We are the yardstick by which all other countries measure themselves.

—Secretary of Labor Lynn Martin, *addressing the 1992 Republican Convention*

Patriots today see government in Washington as an expensive, intrusive institution that limits our freedoms, punishes success, invests in failure and is willing to commit our sons and daughters to far-flung adventures in the name of international comity.

Today's American patriots see many of those who govern as self-serving power brokers, interested less in the public good than in their own political potency.

—Marine Colonel Oliver North, *The Guardian,* July 4, 1995

There was a time when empires were defined by land mass, subjugated peoples, and military might. But the United States is unique because we are an empire of ideals. For two hundred years we have been set apart by our faith in the ideals of democracy, of free men and free markets, and of the extraordinary possibilities that lie within seemingly ordinary men and women. We believe that no power of government is as formidable a force for good as the creativity and entrepreneurial drive of the American people.

—RONALD REAGAN, *addressing the 1992 Republican Convention*

Emerson was right. We are the country of tomorrow. Our revolution did not end at Yorktown. More than two centuries later, America remains on a voyage of discovery, a land that has never become, but is always in the act of becoming.

—RONALD REAGAN, *addressing the 1992 Republican Convention*

Family Values

This is a free country. Within very broad limits, people may live as they wish. And yet, we believe that some ways of living are better than others. Better because they bring more meaning to our lives, to the lives of others, and to our fragile fallible human condition. Marriage and parenthood should be held up because between husband and wife and in fatherhood and motherhood come blessings that cannot be won in any other way.

—FORMER SECRETARY OF EDUCATION WILLIAM J. BENNETT, *addressing the 1992 Republican National Convention*

We refused to assume . . . one of the central obligations of parenthood: to make ourselves the final authority on good and bad, right and wrong, and to take the consequences of what might turn out to be a lifetime battle.

—AUTHOR AND SOCIAL CRITIC MIDGE DECTER, *Liberal Parents, Radical Children*, 1975

The family [is] the first essential cell of human society.

—POPE JOHN XXIII, *Pacem in Terris*, April 10, 1963

Elite opinion—including Bill Clinton—now concedes that Dan Quayle was right: The breakdown of the family is the key to many of America's worst social ills.

—AUTHOR AND POLITICAL COMMENTATOR WILLIAM KRISTOL, *Policy Review*, Winter 1994

Instead of acknowledging the role of the traditional family in sustaining a democratic order, Congress continues at best to ignore, and at worst to undermine, that role in everything from education and health to aging and crime. In addition, Congress has placed new financial pressures on the family. Last year it replaced the Young Child Tax Credit, a Bush-era innovation to provide low-income households a refundable tax credit (about $500 per child) to help them care for newborns and toddlers.

The first and fundamental structure for "human ecology" is the family, in which man receives his first ideas about truth and goodness and learns what it means to love and be loved, and thus what it means to be a person.

—**POPE JOHN PAUL II,** *Centesimus Annus,* 1991

Meanwhile, President Clinton's tax hike—$255 billion over five years—will fall squarely on the American family, both in direct levies and higher prices.

—HENRY HYDE, *Policy Review,* April 1994

Not everyone wants to make the switch toward reliance upon family, community, and mediating institutions, least of all those in government, academia, and grant-receiving organizations whose careers have rested upon the expansion of the public sector at the (literal) expense of the American family. Artificial segregation of issues has, in the past, fostered highly specialized approaches to various problems. On both the right and the left, think tanks are filled with housing wonks and welfare gurus, education experts and economic development eggheads. I'm convinced that the divisions among them were needlessly deepened, if not created in the first place, by the operational divisions within the federal bureaucracy.

—HENRY HYDE, *Roll Call,* January 9, 1995

By profession I am a soldier and take great pride in that fact, but I am prouder, infinitely prouder, to be a father. A soldier destroys in order to build; the father only builds, never destroys. The one has the potentialities of death; the other embodies creation and life. And while the hordes of death are mighty, the battalions of life are mightier still.

—**GENERAL DOUGLAS MACARTHUR,** *Reminiscences,* 1964

Every mother is like Moses. She does not enter the promised land. She prepares the world she will not see.

—**POPE PAUL IV,** *Conversations With Pope Paul,* 1967

When family values are undermined, our country suffers. All too often, parents struggle to instill character in their sons and daughters—only to see their values belittled and their beliefs mocked by those who look down on America. Americans try to raise their children to understand right and wrong—only to be told that every so-called "lifestyle alternative" is morally equivalent. That is wrong.

—**DAN QUAYLE,** *addressing the 1992 Republican Convention*

Our generation's social revolution taught us that family life needs protection. Our laws, policies and society as a whole must support families.

—**MARILYN QUAYLE,** *addressing the 1992 Republican Convention*

Let Freedom Ring

Abstract liberty, like other mere abstractions, is not to be found.

—BRITISH STATESMAN EDMUND BURKE, *Second Speech on Conciliation With America: The Thirteen Resolutions,* March 22, 1775

Freedom and not servitude is the cure of anarchy; as religion, and not atheism, is the true remedy for superstition.

—EDMUND BURKE, *Second Speech on Conciliation With America: The Thirteen Resolutions,* March 22, 1775

Deny them [the colonies] this participation of freedom, and you break that sole bond, which originally made, and must still preserve the unity of the empire.

—EMUND BURKE, *Second Speech on Conciliation With America: The Thirteen Resolution,* March 22, 1775

Fifty years later [after World War II], after change of almost biblical proportions, we know that when freedom grows, America grows. Just as a strong America means a safer world, we have learned that a safer world means a stronger America.

—GEORGE BUSH, *from his speech accepting the Republican nomination,* August 20, 1992

History suggests that capitalism is a necessary condition for political freedom.

—ECONOMIST MILTON FRIEDMAN, *Capitalism and Freedom,* 1962

We Americans understand freedom: we have earned it, we have lived for it, and we have died for it. This nation and its people are freedom's models in a searching world. We can be freedom's missionaries in a doubting world.

—FORMER ARIZONA SENATOR BARRY GOLDWATER, *speaking at the Republican National Convention,* June 16, 1964

Those who seek to live your lives for you, to take your liberty in return for relieving you of yours, those who elevate the state and downgrade the citizen, must see ultimately a world in which earthly power can be substituted for divine will. And this nation was founded upon the rejection of that notion and upon the acceptance of God as the author of freedom.

—BARRY GOLDWATER, June 16, 1964

The genius of the American system is that through freedom we have created extraordinary results from plain old ordinary people.

—SENATOR PHIL GRAMM, 1989

Liberty not only means that the individual has both the opportunity and the burden of choice; it also means that he must bear the consequences of his actions. . . . Liberty and responsibility are inseparable.

—FRIEDRICH HAYEK, NOBEL PRIZE WINNING ECONOMIST AND FREE MARKET ADVOCATE, *The Constitution of Liberty,* 1960

To silence criticism is to silence freedom.

—SOCIAL PHILOSOPHER SIDNEY HOOK, *New York Times Magazine,* September 30, 1951

America's mission to the world did not end when the cold war ended. Our mission is ongoing. Our mission is to continue to tell the world that we are for the freedom and human rights of all men and women, for all time—and to do everything we can transform the ancient dream and hope of freedom into a democratic reality everywhere! And with God's help we will.

—JACK KEMP, November 30, 1990

No man is entitled to the blessings of freedom unless he be vigilant in its preservation.

—GENERAL DOUGLAS MACARTHUR, *in a speech to the people of Japan on the first anniversary of the Japanese constitution,* May 3, 1948

Unless men are free to be vicious they cannot be virtuous.

—**FRANK MEYER,** *In Defense of Freedom: A Conservative Credo,* 1962

No arsenal or no weapon in the arsenals of the world is so formidable as the will and moral courage of free men and women.

—**RONALD REAGAN,** *First Inaugural Address,* January 20, 1981

We will always remember. We will always be proud. We will always be prepared, so we may always be free.

—**RONALD REAGAN,** *on the 40th Anniversary of D-Day, Normandy, France,* June 6, 1984

Freedom is the right to question and change the established way of doing things. It is the continuous revolution of the Market-place. It is the understanding that allows us to recognize shortcomings and seek solutions.

—**RONALD REAGAN,** May 31, 1988

There is no "slippery slope" toward loss of liberties, only a long staircase where each step downward must first be tolerated by the American people and their leaders.

—**ALAN K. SIMPSON,** *The New York Times,* September 26, 1982

My belief has always been . . . that wherever in this land any individual's constitutional rights are being unjustly denied, it is the obligation of the federal government—at the point of bayonet if necessary—to restore that individual's constitutional rights.

—RONALD REAGAN, May 17, 1983

Liberty is the only thing you cannot have unless you are willing to give it to others.

—**PULITZER PRIZE-WINNING NEWSMAN WILLIAM ALLEN WHITE,**
The New York Times

Culture

During a decade of government inattention, raunchy radio personalities such as New York's Howard Stern ceaselessly tested with bawdy banter the limits of how blue they could turn the airwaves.

—**ROBERT H. BORK, SUPREME COURT NOMINEE,** *U.S. News & World Report,*
April 27, 1987

In the area of individual rights the Court, most unexpectedly, has substituted a form of moral philosophy, intellectually thinner than gruel, for the actual principles of the Constitution. It has adopted, almost in haec verba, the radical jurisprudence of today's law schools, i.e., that the individual's right to define himself or herself, particularly in sexual matters, is paramount and that the community has almost no legitimate interests in that area.

—**ROBERT H. BORK,** *National Review,* October 19, 1992

The Ten Commandments are banned from the schoolroom, but pornographic videos are permitted.

—ROBERT H. BORK, *Commentary,* February, 1995

The only question remaining about the decline of Western civilization is the pace.

—ROBERT H. BORK, *National Review,* January 23, 1995

The Christian Coalition speaks for the majority of Americans whose patience has worn thin and who are not disposed to let a half-century go by before reinstating some recognition of religion in those schools where it is wanted. They believe the time has come for a constitutional amendment.

The amendment under consideration would protect "religious expression." In this category would fall a moment of silence in the schools and invocations at public gatherings. Opponents will of course plead the necessity of a "wall" of separation. But they will be hard put to come up with witnesses who will argue persuasively that the passage of such an amendment [permitting school prayer] threatens an established church.

—WILLIAM F. BUCKLEY JR., *The Fresno Bee,* May 12, 1995

Superstition is the religion of feeble minds.

—EDMUND BURKE, *Reflections on the Revolution in France,* 1790

No government has the right to discriminate against any of its own citizens. That's why I support allowing gays in the military. The private behavior of individuals should not be the issue. Rather, the men and women of the armed forces should be judged by how well they perform their jobs.

—**ALFONSE D'AMATO,** *The Arizona Republic,* February 5, 1993

We inhabit a troubled nation beset by violence, broken families, and deteriorating values, where life and living are not so innocent. We are a society failing in self-reliance and self-confidence.

—**ARKANSAS REPRESENTATIVE JAY DICKEY,** August, 1994

The struggle is between the godless people and the people of God and if you want to put it in its basic form, it is between slavery and freedom. I claim we cannot live with these two philosophies in the world forever.

—**BARRY GOLDWATER,** *from a campaign address,* 1964

The conservative movement is founded on the simple tenet that people have the right to live as they please, as long as they don't hurt anyone else in the process. No one has ever shown me how being gay or lesbian harms anyone else.

—**BARRY GOLDWATER,** *The Atlanta Journal and Constitution,* July 19, 1994

The most eloquent prayer is the prayer through hands that heal and bless. The highest form of worship is the worship of unselfish Christian service. The greatest form of praise is the sound of consecrated feet seeking out the lost and helpless.

—**BILLY GRAHAM,** *Evangelical Minister, Chicago American,* April 16, 1967

What is technically possible is not for that very reason morally admissible.

—**VATICAN DOCTRINAL STATEMENT,** *Instruction on Respect for Human Life in its Origin and on the Dignity of Procreation,* March 11, 1987

Markets offer us a vast number of choices, to be sure: and some of those choices are, by any decent ethical measure, morally inferior to others. But it is individual human beings, not some abstraction called "the market," who make those choices, whether it be the choice for instant gratification, for sexual license, for infidelity—or the choice for prudent stewardship of one's money, for sexual responsibility, for faithfulness in friendship, business associations, and marriage.

—**HENRY HYDE,** *National Review,* November 5, 1990

People need religion. It's a vehicle for a moral tradition. A crucial role. Nothing can take its place.

—**EDITOR AND AUTHOR IRVING KRISTOL,** *Two Cheers for Capitalism,* 1979

As conservative evangelical Christians we recognize that ultimately only a nationwide spiritual renewal offers America long-term hope in addressing these moral issues.

—RICHARD D. LAND, *Executive Director of the Christian Life Commission of the Southern Baptist Convention, Policy Review,* January 1993

The religious right are just decent Christians who believe that this country was founded on the basis that the religious could be involved in government. They are simply resisting the notion that religion is a disqualifier for serving in government.

—RUSH LIMBAUGH, *The Door,* November/December 1993

What can explain why 47 percent of Americans, in a recent poll, list as one of the most serious problems faced by the nation the condition of the homeless in our midst? Yet the homeless represent only a tiny fraction of our population. If Americans are as selfish and materialistic as some accuse them of being, why should so many care?

—MICHAEL NOVAK, *Political Commentator and Co-host of Evans & Novak, Forbes,* December 25, 1989

Conservatives should be no more timid about asserting the responsibilities of the individual than they should be about protecting individual rights.

—SUPREME COURT JUSTICE CLARENCE THOMAS, *St. Louis Post-Dispatch*, July 14, 1991

Prosperity

In America, it is freedom that has always attracted explorers and given life to their ideas. Drawn from every corner of the globe, they expect to succeed. Expectancy produces hope. And hope makes all things possible—hope based on a vision not of bricks and mortar but of first principles: the dignity of the individual, private property rights, and opportunity in the free market. Thus the greatness of America is more than the sum total of its force of arms and the opulence of its economy: Its real power is its vision of an unlimited future.

—BARRY ASMUS, *Imprimis,* January 1992

———————————

Envy so often motivates the Left in its quest for redistribution. The economy is not a zero-sum game, and the wealth of a Bill Gates or a Michael Jordan does not take anything away from me. Indeed, the wealth of others enhances my life. Without the generosity of the rich, directly or through the foundations they have established, many of us who prefer life on a university faculty or at a think tank would have had quite different and less satisfying careers.

—**Robert H. Bork,** *National Review,* January 23, 1995

Socialism is the philosophy of failure, the creed of ignorance and the gospel of envy.

—**Winston Churchill,** 1948

When the state promises you security, it impedes, almost inevitably, any chance of your long term success. Because when security becomes your goal, risk is to be avoided; when risk is avoided, growth cannot occur; and when growth is nonexistent, the energies, intelligence and self interest that might have gone into creating wealth—expanding the pie—go instead into dividing it up. Our focus, as a society, shifts from opportunity to entitlement.

—**Theodore J. Forstmann,** *speaking at the Pepperdine University School of Business and Management 1994 Commencement*

Dicky Flatt is an old and dear friend who runs a little print shop in Mexia, Texas. He and his family have worked a lifetime to make a go of their small business and he never quite gets that blue ink off the tips of his fingers. Several years ago, a reporter asked me how I judged the value of government programs. I told her that every time I had to vote on some federal spending program, I asked myself one key question, "Is it worth reaching into Dicky Flatt's pocket to get money to pay for this?" And the answer was—and still is—that there weren't many government programs that could stand up to a test like that.

—**PHIL GRAMM,** *The Houston Chronicle,* May 26, 1993

It is a great paradox of American life that while zealots are hard at work finding new political rights behind every human yearning, constitutional property rights often go unprotected. I suspect that behind this paradox lies a widely held view that economic rights are somehow not very important.

Our Founding Fathers knew better. They recognized that property rights are the most basic of human rights—the rights of human beings to the use and exchange of goods. They also understood that the right to private property is one of freedom's crucial safeguards. It gives citizens the independence they need to criticize their government without having to worry that the government might retaliate by seizing the source of their livelihood.

—**PHIL GRAMM,** *The Washington Times,* October 19, 1993

It is now clear that those who think of the poor only as "victims" dehumanize them. The poor are as capable of responsibility as anybody else. Most of them, in fact, seize normal American opportunities to move out of poverty—as the recent immigrants have done. The rest of us need to believe in their capacities and design our assistance accordingly.

—MICHAEL NOVAK, *Forbes,* December 11, 1989

Recession is when your neighbor loses his job. Depression is when you lose your job. And recovery is when Jimmy Carter loses his.

—RONALD REAGAN, *The New York Times,* October 2, 1986

We're the party that wants to see an America in which people can still get rich.

—RONALD REAGAN, *remarks at a Republican congressional dinner,* May 4, 1982

POLITICS

Politics and Politicians

After all, what does a politician have but his credibility?

—SPIRO T. AGNEW, 1969

The tidal wave of venom that threatens to sweep away the proposal to raise the salaries of Federal officials is flabbergasting. Who would have thought that so many Americans who love incumbent Congressmen so dearly as to award them something resembling life tenure simultaneously hate them so much that they would require them, along with Federal executives and judges, to serve at inadequate and steadily decreasing real compensation?

Political parties are having trouble recruiting good candidates for Congress, and part of the reason most certainly is pay. While salaries in the past 20 years have fallen 30 or 40 percent behind inflation, the price of housing in and around Washington has skyrocketed far past the rate of inflation.

This is also true in many major metropolitan areas. The result is increasing difficultly in recruiting and retaining qualified Federal judges. Many excellent lawyers simply will not consider the Federal bench as a career and many excellent judges are thinking seriously of giving up that career.

—ROBERT H. BORK, *The New York Times,* December 23, 1988

The [Supreme] court is no longer primarily a legal institution but rather a political and cultural power—in one sense, the supreme political and cultural power, because its mandates are difficult to override and will not be ignored or disobeyed.

Perhaps it was inevitable that an institution with such power would come to be viewed as a political prize and a political weapon.

—ROBERT H. BORK, *commenting on why Supreme Court nominations are televised, The New York Times,* June 23, 1993

Political theory sometimes seems an intellectual parlor game, an arena for academic poseurs, with little or no relevance to political reality.

—ROBERT H. BORK, *National Review,* August 9, 1993

The Democrats have feasted on the predicted starvation of American children. A composite of what one has heard and seen on TV is a 6-year-old girl looking through the window of a restuarant, a tear in her eye. It makes absolutely no difference that the statisticians can predict that next year the amount of food given to children by an arm of government in the form of school lunches will increase by 4.5 percent. The Democrats would much rather project pictures of starving children than keep children from starving, provided they can blame the Republicans.

—WILLIAM F. BUCKLEY JR., *National Review*, May 1, 1995

Politicians aren't philosophers, and in that sense expedience is, so to speak, what they do. But it is disorienting to lose all contact with the illumination of philosophy.

—WILLIAM F. BUCKLEY JR., *The National Review*, May 1, 1995

What we saw on display before that Senate committee [hearing on the Whitewater scandal] was an ethos of evasiveness and a real culture of deceit. Josh Steiner's alarm rings as true as it can. It's an honest account. And his testimony rings false as it can be. I think what's happened to these people is they won this election. They think they got this game down cold and therefore they got a certain contempt for the truth and I think a contempt for the public. These were outstanding hearings, incidentally, by the

Senate committee. They did a tremendous job. And I think it is utterly devastating for the Clinton White House.

—PATRICK BUCHANAN, *The McLaughlin Group,* August 6, 1994

Politics are almost as exciting as war, and quite as dangerous. In war you can only be killed once, but in politics many times.

—WINSTON CHURCHILL, 1920

As long as there are only 3 to 4 people on the floor, the country is in good hands. It's only when you have 50 to 60 in the Senate that you want to be concerned.

—KANSAS SENATOR ROBERT DOLE, *The New York Times,* May 9, 1985

And Bill Clinton, I want to thank you for doubling the size of our audience here today. I am convinced the President is going to do his part in clearing up the number one problem we had in the 1992 campaign. The Democrats won the election in 1992 because they were able to confuse the American people as to who they were and what they stood for. And we lost the election for exactly the same reason. We confused the American people as to who we were and what we stood for. Bill Clinton has already corrected the first half of the problem, and the question is, can we correct the second half? I say yes.

—**PHIL GRAMM,** *speaking to the Conservative Political Action Conference in Washington, D.C.,* February 18, 1993

Politicians all too often are eager to invest taxpayer's money in the next election, but almost never in the next generation.

—**PHIL GRAMM,** *The Houston Chronicle,* June 15, 1993

A mandatory revolving door for elected officials would only strengthen the grip of the permanent bureaucracy. Representative government would be the loser.

—**HENRY HYDE,** *discussing mandatory term limits, Chicago Sun-Times,* July 16, 1994

Democracy itself cannot indefinitely survive public cynicism and contempt. Contempt for the Congress will inevitably become contempt for the rule of law. The first task of this 102nd Congress, then, is to restore a measure of the people's confidence in their institutions of government.

—**HENRY HYDE,** *Roll Call,* December 3, 1990

I have been covering politics all my adult life, and I confess my own inability to propose reforms that would have a realistic chance of becoming law. The idea of term limitation strikes me as a bad idea—there is far more turnover in Congress than most critics realize.

—COLUMNIST JAMES KILPATRICK, *on political reform, The Atlanta Journal and Constitution,* May 24, 1991

Poor old Constitution! If members of the House and Senate have their way, at least 19 amendments, 18 too many, will be added to the fundamental law of our land. Obviously members came to Washington well prepared. They introduced more than 70 resolutions on the opening day of Congress. Since then a dozen more have appeared. None of them is likely to pass, and only a few will ever get to committee hearings. The republic will survive.

—COLUMNIST JAMES KILPATRICK, *The Atlanta Journal and Constitution,* March 17, 1993

A government is not legitimate merely because it exists.

—FORMER U.N. REPRESENTATIVE JEANE KIRKPATRICK, *commenting on the Sandinista government in Nicaragua, Time,* June 17, 1985

There'e an old saying: Never strike a king unless you kill him. In politics you don't hit your opponent unless you knock him out.

—**RICHARD M. NIXON,** *The Saturday Evening Post,* February 25, 1967

For years politician have promised the moon—I'm the first one to be able to deliver it.

—**RICHARD M. NIXON,** 1969

If an individual wants to be a leader and isn't controversial, that means he never stood for anything.

—**RICHARD M. NIXON,** *Dallas Times Herald,* December 10, 1978

I have learned that one of the most important rules in politics is poise—which means looking like an owl after you have behaved like a jackass.

—**RONALD REAGAN,** August 9, 1973

Professional politicians like to talk about the value of experience in government. Nuts! The only experience you gain in politics is how to be political.

—**RONALD REAGAN,** *from a 1976 speech*

There were so many candidates on the platform that there were not enough promises to go around.

—**RONALD REAGAN,** *on the Democratic presidential primary debate in New Hampshire, Newsweek,* February 6, 1984

The nine most terrifying words on the English language are, "I'm from the government and I'm here to help."

—**RONALD REAGAN,** August 12, 1986

Politics is supposed to be the second oldest profession. I have come to realize that it bears a very close resemblance to the first.

—**RONALD REAGAN,** *speech at a business conference in Los Angeles, California,* March 2, 1994

It is not the business of politicians to please everyone.

—**MARGARET THATCHER,** 1978

There are two ways of making a Cabinet. One way is to have in it people representing the differenct points of view within the party, within the broad philosophy. The other way is to have in it only the people who want to go in the direction which every instinct tells me we have to go: clearly, steadily, firmly, with resolution. As Prime Minister, I could not waste my time having internal arguments.

—**MARGARET THATCHER,** 1979

The impact of 12 years of both parties blaming each other and of both ends of Pennsylvania Avenue blaming each other is debilitating to the country and to the process, to the institution of the presidency, to the institution of the Congress.

—**VIN WEBER,** *head of Empower, a conservative think tank and former U.S. Representative, Time,* June 8, 1992

Conservatives on Conservatives

Conservative: A statesman who is enamored of existing evils, as distinguished from the Liberal, who wishes to replace them with others.

—**JOURNALIST AMBROSE BIERCE,** *The Devil's Dictionary,* 1978

There are those who say that conservatives must make a choice between a message of economic growth and one of cultural renewal. Take your side, we are told, and the fight can begin. Make your decision between economics and cultural values.

This choice is false; this conflict is destructive; and this decision, if forced on conservatives, would come at an unacceptable cost to their coalition. It is false in the realm of ideas because it ignores the full range of human needs, and costly in the realm of politics because it undermines the coalition of conscience that could transform the nation and renew its culture.

—JACK KEMP, *USA Today* Magazine, May, 1995

The intelligent conservative combines a disposition to preserve with an ability to reform.

—RUSSELL KIRK, *Columnist and Founding Editor of National Review, Intelligent Woman's Guide to Conservatism,* 1957

The twentieth-century conservative is concerned, first of all, for the regeneration of spirit and character—with the perennial problem of the inner order of the soul, the restoration of the ethical understanding, and the religious sanction upon which any life worth living is founded. This is conservatism at its highest.

—RUSSELL KIRK, *The Conservative Mind,* 1953

A welfare state, properly conceived, can be an integral part of a conservative society.

—EDITOR AND AUTHOR IRVING KRISTOL, *American Spectator,* 1977

His [Reagan's] posture was forward-looking, his accent was on economic growth rather than sobriety. All those Republicans with the hearts and souls of accountants—the traditional ideological curse of the party—were nervous, even dismayed.

—IRVING KRISTOL, *Reflections of a Neo-Conservative,* 1983

[A neoconservative] is a liberal who has been mugged by reality.

—IRVING KRISTOL, *Two Cheers for Capitalism,* 1978

[The Founding Fathers] understood that republican self-government could not exist if humanity did not possess . . . the traditional "republican virtues" of self-control, self-reliance, and a disinterested concern for the public good.

—IRVING KRISTOL, *Reflections of a Neo-Conservative,* 1993

In assembling a staff, the conservative leader faces a greater problem than does the liberal. In general, liberals want more government and hunger to be the ones running it. Conservatives want less government and want no part of it. Liberals want to run other people's lives. Conservatives want to be left alone to run their own lives . . . Liberals flock to government; conservatives have to be enticed and persuaded. With a smaller field to choose from, the conservative leader often has to choose between those who are loyal and not bright and those who are bright but not loyal.

—RICHARD M. NIXON, *Leaders,* 1994

We're not winning because we hide who we are. We're winning because we advertise who we are. We don't have to pretend to be mainstream. We are mainstream.

—RALPH REED, *Executive Director of the Christian Coalition, The Times Union,* November 12, 1994

Liberals

Ultraliberalism today translates into a whimpering isolationism in foreign policy, a mulish obstructionism in domestic policy, and a pusillanimous pussyfooting on the ciritical issue of law and order.

—SPIRO T. AGNEW, *Springfield, Illinois,* September 10, 1970

There is one way to tell the liberals and conservatives apart at a glance. On picking up a book on constitutional theory—if, for some reason, you should wish to do that—look for the animating catchphrase. If the author says "moral reasoning," he is a liberal; if he says "natural law," he is a conservative.

—ROBERT H. BORK, *National Review,* February 7, 1994

How can the modern relativist exercise tolerance if he doesn't believe in anything to begin with? It is not hard to exhibit tolerance toward a point of view if you have no point of view of your own with which that point of view conflicts.

—WILLIAM F. BUCKLEY JR., *Up From Liberalism,* 1959

Modern liberalism, for most liberals is not a consciously understood set of rational beliefs, but a bundle of unexamined prejudices and conjoined sentiments. The basic ideas and beliefs seem more satisfactory when they are not made fully explicit, when they merely lurk rather obscurely in the background, coloring the rhetoric and adding a certain emotive glow.

—EDITOR AND AUTHOR JAMES BURNHAM, *Suicide of the West,* 1985

Fellow Americans, the liberals just don't get it. They don't understand—we can't create more employees without creating more employers. We can't have capitalism without capital.

—JACK KEMP, *addressing the 1992 Republican Convention*

[Bill Clinton] says he wants to tax the rich, but, folks, he defines rich—as anyone who has a job. You've heard of the separations of powers. My opponent practices a different theory: "The power of separations." Government has the power to separate you from your wallet.

—**GEORGE BUSH,** August 20, 1992

When Marxist dictators shoot their way into power in Central America, the San Francisco Democrats don't blame the guerrillas and their Soviet allies, they blame United States policies of one hundred years ago, but then they always blame America first.

—JEANE KIRKPATRICK, *address to the 1984 Republican Convention*

A liberal is one who says it's all right for an 18-year-old girl to perform in a pornographic movie as long as she gets paid minimum wage.

—IRVING KRISTOL, *Two Cheers for Capitalism,* 1979

Whenever a Republican leaves one side of the aisle and goes to the other, it raises the intelligence quotient of both parties.

—CLARE BOOTHE LUCE, 1956

At the core of liberalism is the spoiled child—miserable, as all spoiled children are, unsatisfied, demanding, ill-disciplined, despotic, and useless. Liberalism is a philosophy of sniveling brats.

—P. J. O'ROURKE, *Parliament of Whores,* 1991

The gap between us and our opponents is a cultural divide. It is not just a difference between conservative and liberal; it is a difference between fighting for what is right and refusing to see what is wrong.

—**DAN QUAYLE,** *addressing the 1992 Republican Convention*

Republicans believe every day is the Fourth of July, but Democrats believe every day is April 15.

—**RONALD REAGAN,** *The New York Times,* October 10, 1984

A friend of mine was asked to a costume ball a short time ago. He slapped some egg on his face and went as a liberal economist.

—**RONALD REAGAN,** February 11, 1988

The end of the energy crisis made some Americans, mostly liberals, very sad because it had been a grand excuse to boss people around—telling them what and how fast to drive, where to set their thermostats, how to construct buildings, etc.

—**GEORGE WILL,** *The Buffalo News,* June 26, 1995

War and Peace

It's not the credibility of the United states, it's the credibility of Bill Clinton. This anti-American demagogue Aristide is not worth the life of a single United States Marine. Where in the constitution does Bill Clinton get the authority to take us to war against a nation that has done nothing whatsoever to the United States of America?

—**PATRICK BUCHANAN,** *commenting on the possible invasion of Haiti, The McLaughlin Group,* August 6, 1994

Armaments do not, generally speaking, cause wars. This notion, the logical crux of all arguments in favor of disarmament, turns the casual relationship upside down. Actually, it is wars or conflicts threatening war, that cause armaments, not the reverse.

—**JAMES BURNHAM,** *Founding Editor of National Review, The War We Are In,* 1967

A prisoner of war is a man who tries to kill you and fails, and then asks you not to kill him.

—**WINSTON CHURCHILL,** 1952

People of Western Europe: A landing was made this morning on the coast of France by troops of the Allied Expeditionary Force. This landing is part of the concerted United Nations plan for the liberation of Europe, made in conjunction with our great Russian allies. I call upon all who love freedom to stand with us now. Together we shall achieve victory.

—**DWIGHT D. EISENHOWER,** *from his D-Day radio broadcast,* June 6, 1944

In the final choice the soldier's pack is not so heavy as the prisoner's chains.

—DWIGHT D. EISENHOWER, 1953

We cannot allow the American flag to be shot at anywhere on earth if we are to retain our respect and prestige.

—BARRY GOLDWATER, August 1964

Even in a world where the lion and the lamb are about to lie down together, it is very important that the United States of America be the lion.

—PHIL GRAMM, November 9, 1994

I have grave doubts that when this whole episode is over, the good guys and the bad guys in Haiti will have been separated out and there is going to be a happy solution. . . . I did not support the invasion and I do not support the occupation. If we stay in Haiti long enough and get deeply involved in this conflict, Americans are going to die in Haiti.

—PHIL GRAMM, *Defense News,* September 26, 1994

I have been opposed to the War Powers Act as an unconstitutional infringement on the authority of the president ever since I was first elected to Congress in 1974. Having watched the War Powers Resolution in operation over the past 20 years, I have become convinced that it is not merely unconstitutional, but also profoundly unwise and dangerous.

—HENRY HYDE, *The Washington Times,* May 24, 1995

The nuclear crisis in North Korea worries most Americans. But, those living in Hawaii, Alaska and on the Pacific Coast ought to be the most alarmed. For in addition to enlarging its nuclear weapons capacity, the renegade regime is rapidly developing sophisticated missiles to hurl those weapons well beyond the horizons of the Korean Peninsula. Honolulu, Anchorage and Seattle are not yet within reach, but our defense planners are fools if they cannot envision the day when they will be.

—HENRY HYDE, *on North Korea's nuclear threat, The Washington Times,* August 29, 1994

We lost sight of one of the cardinal maxims of guerrilla war—the guerrilla wins if he does not lose, the conventional army loses if it does not win.

—HENRY KISSINGER, *Foreign Affairs* magazine, 1968

You can't win through negotiations what you can't win on the battlefield.

—HENRY KISSINGER, 1973

It is fatal to enter any war without the will to win it.

—GENERAL DOUGLAS MACARTHUR, *1952 Republican National Convention*

History teaches that wars begin when governments believe the price of aggression is cheap.

—RONALD REAGAN, January 16, 1984

To blame the military for war makes about as much sense as suggesting that we get rid of cancer by getting rid of doctors.

—RONALD REAGAN, June 7, 1970.

I call upon the scientific community in our country, those who gave us nuclear weapons, to turn their great talents now to the cause of mankind and world peace, to give us the means of rendering those nuclear weapons impotent and obsolete.

—RONALD REAGAN, March 23, 1983

Mr. President

Bill Clinton's election is likely to hurt America in many ways: the appointment of liberal judicial activists to the Supreme Court, an Environmental Protection Agency run amok, and a return to Carter-era tax policies.

—TEXAS REPRESENTATIVE DICK ARMEY, *Policy Review,* January 1993

All too often, President Clinton has signaled right then turned left, which only results in disaster.

—MISSOURI SENATOR JOHN ASHCROFT, *The New York Times,* January 25, 1995

The Clinton health care plan will massively expand the power and reach of the "nanny state"; it represents the largest power grab by the federal government in recent history.

—WILLIAM J. BENNETT, *on Bill Clinton's health care plan, The Washington Times,* November 15, 1993

As they contemplate the approaching Clinton presidency, its style, and its policy initiatives, conservatives may wish to consider the advantages of catacombs. Despite his campaign rhetoric, President Clinton's administration seems likely to be more liberal than the administrations of Walter Mondale or Michael Dukakis would have been. Conservatives will have little chance of stopping some of the new president's initiatives; some we may be able to moderate; and some will die in the face of reality.

—**ROBERT H. BORK,** *Policy Review,* January 1993

Clinton's problem is even though he's an Arkansas governor from a conservative state in the South, has allowed himself to become the surrogate for a cultural elite and a political elite, both of which are despised by the American people. There are two major currents, I think, to this anti-Washington move, among others. One of them is the cultural war, which has gone all through the South, Texas and areas like that. Out in the West it is issues of land, of guns, of property rights; ranchers, miners, loggers, people like that despite the regulations that are coming out of Washington, D.C. There's a new sagebrush rebellion building and it's against Bill Clinton.

—**PATRICK BUCHANAN,** *The McLaughlin Group,* August 20, 1994

President Clinton has turned in the right direction. But before he can seriously engage the attention of serious men, he has to submit to certain disciplines, like learning the alphabet and the multiplication tables, and weighing words that seem endlessly to come from a forked tongue.

—**WILLIAM F. BUCKLEY JR.,** *The Cincinnati Enquirer,* June 22, 1995

I believe the second half of the 20th century will be known as the age of Nixon.

—**ROBERT DOLE,** *at the funeral of Richard M. Nixon, Washington Times,*
April 28, 1994

There are no easy matters that will ever come to you as President. If they are easy they will be settled at a lower level.

—**DWIGHT D. EISENHOWER,** *advice to John F. Kennedy*

This desk of mine is one at which a man may die, but from which he cannot resign.

—**DWIGHT D. EISENHOWER,** *Parade* Magazine, February 2, 1958

I have one yardstick by which I test every major problem—and that yardstick is: Is it good for America?

—**DWIGHT D. EISENHOWER,** April 16, 1956

There is one thing about being president. Nobody can tell you when to sit down.

—**DWIGHT D. EISENHOWER,** 1953

Unlike presidential administrations, problems rarely have terminal dates.

—**DWIGHT D. EISENHOWER,** *State of the Union Address,* January 12, 1961

Few events touch the heart of every American as profoundly as the death of a president—for the president is our leader, and every American feels that he knows him in a special way because he hears his voice so often, glimpses his picture in the paper, sees him on television, and so we all mourn his loss and feel that our world will be a lonelier place without him.

—BILLY GRAHAM, *at the funeral of Richard M. Nixon,* April 28, 1994

If a budget is a statement of political priorities, then, presidential rhetoric notwithstanding, fighting crime clearly doesn't rank very high on the Clinton agenda.

—PHIL GRAMM, *quoted in The Washington Times,* May 10, 1994

Judging from the president's addiction to spending tax dollars on emergency boathouses, emergency swimming pools, emergency soccer fields and emergency graffiti abatement, it's not difficult to understand why so many of this administration's goals have as much chance of coming true as a hog has of sprouting wings and soaring with eagles.

—PHIL GRAMM, *USA Today,* April 20, 1993

George Bush has continued the Reagan reform of the federal judiciary. By appointing Clarence Thomas to the Supreme Court, and by sticking with him in the face of ruthless assault on

Thomas' integrity, the president not only put an articulate conservative on the nation's highest bench; he also strengthened those millions of African-Americans who are tired of living on the liberal plantation.

—**HENRY HYDE,** *on George Bush, Star Tribune,* March 23, 1992

The Clinton administration's problems haven't been communications problems. They've been policy problems.

—**HENY HYDE,** *The Washington Post,* June 4, 1993

Bill Clinton's low standing with the American people is not the Democrats' real problem. He is not an aberrant or dissident Democrat whose policies and appointments run counter to the soul of his party. On the contrary, he perfectly represents the ideological mainstream of that party. That is its problem.

—**HENRY HYDE,** *The Washington Times,* November 8, 1994

Presidents rarely have the luxury of making easy decisions. By definition, when an issue reaches the Oval Office, its resolution will demand trade-offs among competing objectives.

—**HENRY KISSINGER,** *The Washington Post,* June 6, 1994

He came into office when the forces of history were moving America from a position of dominance to one of leadership.

Dominance reflects strength; leadership must be earned. And Richard Nixon earned that leadership role for his country with courage, dedication and skill.

—HENRY KISSINGER, *in his eulogy for Richard M. Nixon, The Washington Times,* April 28, 1994

Richard Nixon's greatest accomplishment was as much moral as it was political: to lead from strength at a moment of apparent weakness, to husband a nation's resilience and thus to lay the basis for victory in the Cold War.

—HENRY KISSINGER, *Washington Times,* April 28, 1994

Statesmen who base their policy on the expectation of recurrent miracles usually suffer shipwreck.

—HENRY KISSINGER, *Newsweek,* September 27, 1993

The presidency has many problems, but boredom is the least of them.

—RICHARD M. NIXON, January 9, 1973

I have never thought much of the notion that the presidency makes a man presidential. What has given the American presidency its vitality is that each man remains distinctive. His abilities become more obvious, and his faults become more glaring. The presidency is not a finishing school. It is a magnifying glass.

—RICHARD M. NIXON, *Memoirs,* 1978

Certainly in the next 50 years we shall see a woman president, perhaps sooner than you think. A woman can and should be able to do any political job that a man can do.

—RICHARD M. NIXON, *in a speech to the League of Women Voters,*
Washington D.C., April 16, 1969

When presidents begin to worry about images . . . they become like athletes, the football teams and the rest, who become so concerned about what is written about them and what is said about them that they don't play the game well . . . The President, with the enormous responsibilities he has, must not be constantly preening in front of a mirror. I don't' worry about polls, I don't worry about images. I never have.

—RICHARD M. NIXON, 1971

I've often wondered how some people on positions of this kind . . . manage without having any acting experience.

—RONALD REAGAN, *in an interview with Barbara Walters on ABC-TV,*
March 24, 1986

I think the presidency is an institution over which you have temporary custody.

—**RONALD REAGAN,** *responding to a question about what he would tell students about the presidency, Time,* April 7, 1986

In our America, most people still believed in the power of a better tomorrow. So together, we got the government off the backs of the American people. We created millions of new jobs for Americans at all income levels. We cut taxes and freed the people from the shackles of too much government. As a result, the economy burst loose in the longest peacetime expansion ever. We brought America back—bigger and better than ever.

—**RONALD REAGAN,** *Growth, Opportunity, Prosperity: Setting The Record Straight on the '80s*

What [Bill Clinton] has failed to grasp is that the American people voted for Clinton in 1992 because he campaigned as a New Democrat, an outsider promising to bring a fresh agenda to Washington. But since taking office, the President has allowed himself to be coopted by the only institution in Washington that was less popular than the Bush Administration—the Democratic Congress. Instead of pursuing the New Democrat policies he campaigned on, he has delivered Old Democrat policies that had been held up by gridlock for 12 years. In that way I suppose Clinton has been emulating LBJ.

—VIN WEBER, *head of Empower, a Conservative think tank, and former U.S. Representative, National Review,* December 27, 1993

Since taking office, the Clinton Administration has essentially abdicated its leadership responsibilities on the world stage, creating a power vacuum. With nobody steering the ship of state, others have moved in.

—VIN WEBER, *National Review,* November 15, 1993

The Media

A tiny and closed fraternity of privileged men, elected by no one, and enjoying a monopoly sanctioned and licensed by government.

—SPIRO T. AGNEW, November 13, 1969

First radio, then television, have assaulted and overturned the privacy of the home, the real American privacy, which permitted the development of a higher and more independent life within democratic society. Parents can no longer control the atmosphere of the home and have lost even the will to do so. With great subtlety and energy, television enters not only the room, but also the tastes of old and young alike, appealing to the immediately pleasant and subverting whatever does not confrom to it.

—**ALLAN BLOOM,** *The Closing of the American Mind,* 1987

In Washington, if a rumor is sustained long enough, it eventually spills into the press and becomes credible. And it becomes damning.

—**ROBERT H. BORK,** *The Washington Post,* October 5, 1987

Saying the *Washington Post* is just a newspaper is like saying Rasputin was just a country priest.

—**PATRICK BUCHANAN,** 1986

A bullpen seething with mischief.

—**GEORGE BUSH,** *commenting on reporters covering the vice presidential campaign, The New York Times,* October 7, 1984

It is better to be making the news than taking it, to be an actor rather than a critic.

—**WINSTON CHURCHILL,** 1898

I don't attempt to be a poker player before this crowd.

—**DWIGHT D. EISENHOWER,** April 30, 1958

Well, when you come down to it, I don't see that a reporter could do much to a president, do you?

—DWIGHT D. EISENHOWER, *The New York Times,* August 9, 1964

I won't say that the papers misquote me, but I sometimes wonder where Christianity would be today if some of those reporters had been Matthew, Mark, Luke, and John.

—BARRY GOLDWATER, *The New York Times,* August 11, 1964

God help us, you're a rotten bunch!

—BARRY GOLDWATER, 1974

Whatever else can be said for or against our national media, their attention span is short: and so public life moves on.

—HENRY HYDE, *National Review,* April 30, 1990

The press is like the peculiar uncle you keep in the attic—just one of those unfortunate things.

—G. GORDON LIDDY, *Watergate Participant, Newsweek,* January 12, 1987

An expert is somebody who is more than 50 miles away from home, has no responsibility for implementing the advice he gives, and shows slides.

—EDWIN MEESE 3RD, *The New York Times,* January 24, 1984

I've never canceled a subscription to a newspaper because of bad cartoons or editorials. If that were the case, I wouldn't have any newspapers or magazines to read.

—**RICHARD M. NIXON,** *NBC-TV,* April 8, 1984

People in the media say they must look . . . at the president with a microscope, but boy, when they use a proctoscope, that's going too far.

—**RICHARD M. NIXON,** *NBC-TV,* April 8, 1984

I, and others in my party, must be constantly aware of the higher standard to which we are being held—and live up to it. Anyone who has had the nation's press corps camped on his front lawn for months on end—as my family and I have—should know that.

—**OLIVER NORTH,** *The Washington Post,* March 24, 1993

There's good journalism and there's bad journalism. And I want to say something to you good journalists. You are being overwhelmed by the bad journalism and the bad journalists of America.

—**DAN QUAYLE,** *The New York Times,* August 13, 1992

You fellas are going to call me whatever you want to call me, but I have a hunch it's going to be "front runner."

—**RONALD REAGAN,** *after his victory in the New Hampshire primary,* 1980

A reader should be able to identify a column without its byline or funny little picture on top—purely by look or feel, or its turgidity ratio.

—**WILLIAM SAFIRE,** *Vanity Fair,* September 1984 *(Quoted by Robert H. Yoakman)*

The higher the classification [of secrecy], the quicker you'll report it.

—**SECRETARY OF STATE GEORGE P. SCHULTZ,** *The New York Times,* October 3, 1986

[Democratic nations] must try to find ways to starve the terrorist and the hijacker of the oxygen of publicity on which they depend.

—**MARGARET THATCHER,** July 15, 1985

I often felt that the media assumed that, to be black, one had to espouse leftist ideas and Democratic politics. Any black who deviated from the ideological litany of requisites was an oddity and was to be cut from the herd and attacked. Hence, any disagreement we had with black Democrats or those on the Left was exaggerated. Our character and motives were impugned and challenged by the same reporters who supposedly were writing objective stories. In fact, on numerous occasions, I have found myself debating and arguing with a reporter, who had long since closed his notebook, put away his pen, and turned off his tape recorder.

—CLARENCE THOMAS, *Policy Review,* October 1991

They kill good trees to put out bad newspapers.

—SECRETARY OF THE INTERIOR JAMES G. WATT, *Newsweek,* March 8, 1982

GOVERNMENT

The Role of Government

The ostensibly compassionate policies of the state have ruined our inner cities and dehumanized their beneficiaries. Whatever the issue—public education, the sanctity of human life, the criminal justice system, job creation in the private sector—the legacy of the ever-expanding state is one of lost freedom, weaker families, and few jobs.

—**BILL BAKER,** *California Representative,* July, 1994

National power has been expanded at the expense of the states. The federal government is too big, too intrusive and too involved in matters over which it has no legitimate responsibility. Federal courts no longer defend the rights of states, so legislators must be sensitive to principles of federalism or the states will disappear.

—**ROBERT H. BORK,** *The Washington Times,* March 9, 1995

I think the mood of the American people is rancorous, it is populist and it is nationalist. And you see its manifestation not only in the mood to put term limits on all politicians, but maybe even on judges. You see it in these efforts at direct democracy, of people trying to take back into their own hands and write laws themselves. They're putting on tax limits, they're putting on spending limits, they're overturning gay rights ordinances. I think what's happening, John, is the tremendous distrust of Washington, D.C. that's been building for decades now is approaching critical mass.

—PATRICK BUCHANAN, *The McLaughlin Group,* August 20, 1994

The government of the United States, under Lyndon Johnson, proposes to concern itself over the quality of American life. And this is something very new in the political theory of free nations. The quality of life has heretofore depended on the quality of human beings who gave tone to that life, and they were its priests and its poets, not its bureaucrats.

—WILLIAM F. BUCKLEY JR., *National Review,* August 7, 1965

The state is a divine institution. Without it we have anarchy, and the lawlessness of anarchy is counter to the natural law; so we abjure all political theories which view the state as inherently and necessarily evil. But it is the state which has been in history the principal instrument of abuse of the people, and so it is central to the conservatives; program to keep the state from accumulating any but the most necessary powers.

—WILLIAM F. BUCKLEY JR., *The Catholic World*

I should sooner live in a society governed by the first two thousand names in the Boston telephone directory than in a society governed by two thousand faculty members of Harvard University.

—WILLIAM F. BUCKLEY JR., *Rumbles*

Your representative owes you, not his industry only, but his judgment; and he betrays instead of serving you if he sacrifices it to your opinion.

—EDMUND BURKE *from his speech to the Electors of Bristol,* November 3, 1774

All government indeed, every human benefit and enjoyment, every virtue and every prudent act is founded on compromise and barter.

—BRITISH STATESMAN EDMUND BURKE, *from Second Speech on Conciliation with America: The Thirteen Resolutions,* March 22, 1775

Government is a contrivance of human wisdom to provide for human wants. Men have a right that these wants should be provided for by this wisdom.

—EDMUND BURKE, *Reflections on the Revolution in France*, 1792

When I met with President Gorbachev last July, we talked about perestroika and its impact on the Soviet economy. Had I described our American public housing system to him he probably would have prescribed a good dose of restructuring. And Gorby would be right. Like the Soviet economy, our public housing system is a morass of complicated regulations, perverse incentives, confused jurisdictional lines, and bureaucratic lethargy.

But the worst part is that the system doesn't really work. It doesn't provide decent housing to many residents, and it still costs the taxpayers a boatload of money.

—ALFONSE D'AMATO, *Roll Call*, February 26, 1990

Our best protection against bigger government in Washington is better government in the states.

—DWIGHT D. EISENHOWER, June 8, 1964

Call me a heretic in the Jeffersonian temple, but it must be said: Democracy isn't synonymous with liberty. In the past 100 years, the expansion of the electorate has kept pace with the decline of individual freedom. For a third of our working lives, we are serfs of the state. If self-employed, our enterprises are minutely regulated. Government has a near monopoly on the education of our children, a position it uses to subvert parental values. We can't operate a vegetable stand, build a porch on our house, keep a sidearm for self-defense, own a mutt or go fishing without Big Brother's express permission.

—DON FEDER, *Washington Times,* September 19, 1994

Most of the energy of political work is devoted to correcting the effects of mismanagement of government.

—MILTON FRIEDMAN, *PBS, Firing Line,* October 9, 1988

Nothing is so permanent as a temporary government program.

—MILTON FRIEDMAN, *Attributed*

Governments never learn. Only people learn.

—MILTON FRIEDMAN, *Attributed*

I think the entire approach to federally controlled and federally dominated bureaucracies designed to impose middle class bureaucrats on the poor has now failed, and I think that we need from the ground up to look at all of them.

—**NEWT GINGRICH**, *I, Newt: The Quotations of Speaker Gingrich*, 1994

The answer is not more government—it's more opportunity. And the path to greater opportunity for all our people will be found by controlling federal spending and letting the people who do the work, pay the taxes and pull the wagon keep more of what they earn.

—**PHIL GRAMM**, *addressing the 1992 Republican Convention*

All over the world people are rejecting government as a decision maker. All over the world people are rejecting government as a source of wisdom, a source of prosperity or a source of efficiency. All over the world people are turning to individual freedom and free enterprise and individual initiative.

—**PHIL GRAMM**, January 31, 1993

I know many people are going to be disappointed in what we do, but what we are going to do is we are going to begin to make government smaller.

—**PHIL GRAMM**, *USA Today,* November 14, 1994

The greatest danger to liberty today comes from the men who are most needed and most powerful in modern government, namely, the efficient expert administrators exclusively concerned with what they regard as public good.

—ECONOMIST FRIEDRICH HAYEK, *The Consitution of Liberty,* 1960

I was guilty of judging capitalism by its operations and socialism by its hopes and aspirations; capitalism by its works and socialism by its literature.

—SOCIAL PHILOSOPHER SIDNEY HOOK, *Out of Step,* 1988

We believe that as our country moves into a new economic era, the top-heavy model of government must yield to a decentralized one in which government equips citizens to solve their own problems. So it's not surprising that advocates of such an empowerment strategy have faced stiff resistance from members of their own parties—Democrats from big-government liberals who still believe that there is a government solution for every problem and Republicans from anti-government conservatives who believe that the best government role is none at all.

—JACK KEMP, *Austin American-Statesman,* July 4, 1995

What is self government about, after all? What is this society about? They certainly are not about producing a utopia through the instrument of the state. Even if government could produce all that it promises, we would not want those results on the terms they are offered. They are terms that require that we surrender a good that is more important than good results: our freedom to make choices.

—**ALAN L. KEYS,** *former U.S. Senatorial (R) Candidate from Maryland, Imprimis,* October 1992

Poverty and Suffering are not due to the unequal distribution of goods and resources, but to the unequal distribution of capitalism.

—**RUSH LIMBAUGH,** *Policy Review,* Summer 1992

I have come up with a new national symbol for the United States. I think we need to junk the eagle and come up with a symbol that is more appropriate for the kind of government we have today. We need to replace the eagle with a huge sow that has a lot of nipples and a bunch of fat little piglets hanging on them, all trying to suckle as much nourishment from them as possible.

—**RUSH LIMBAUGH,** *The Way Things Ought to Be,* 1992

Free enterprise suggests that the economic system can work all alone, in a political vacuum. That is not so. Unstable or unsound political regimes can destroy economic growth. Moreover, in or own history, political acts have been immensely creative for economic growth.

—**MICHAEL NOVAK,** *Political Commentator and co-host of Evans and Novak, Forbes,*
August 7, 1989

If you think health care is expensive now, wait until you see what it costs when it's free.

—**P. J. O'ROURKE,** *address to the CATO Institute,* 1993

Giving money and power to government is like giving whiskey and car keys to teenage boys.

—**P. J. O'ROURKE,** *Parliament of Whores,* 1992

Where self-interest is suppressed, it is replaced by a burdensome system of bureaucratic control that dries up the wellsprings of initiative and creativity.

—**POPE JOHN PAUL II,** *Centesimus Annus*

Once upon a time, the only contact with government was when you went to buy a stamp.

—**RONALD REAGAN,** 1965

Too many people, especially in government, feel that the nearest thing to eternal life we will ever see on this earth is a government program.

—RONALD REAGAN, May 10, 1972

Govenment does not solve problems; it subsidizes them.

—RONALD REAGAN, December 11, 1972

It is not my intention to do away with government. It is rather to make it work—work with us, not over us; stand by our side, not ride on our back. Government can and must provide opportunity, not smother it; foster productivity, not stifle it.

—RONALD REAGAN, January 20, 1981

Government has an important role in helping develop a country's economic foundation. But the critical test is whether government is genuinely working to liberate individuals by creating incentives to work, save, invest, and succeed.

—RONALD REAGAN, October 30, 1981

Government is the people's business and every man, woman and child becomes a shareholder with the first penny of tax paid.

—RONALD REAGAN, January 14, 1982

Government's view of the economy could be summed up in a few short phrases: If it moves, tax it. If it keeps moving, regulate it. And if it stops moving, subsidize it.

—**RONALD REAGAN,** August 15, 1986

The Balanced Budget

Not all spending initiatives were designed to be immortal.

—**GEORGE BUSH,** February 9, 1989

As quickly as you start spending federal money in large amounts, it looks like free money.

—**DWIGHT D. EISENHOWER,** February 9, 1955

The reason Congress hasn't balanced the budget is that the sky hasn't fallen lately.

—**REPRESENTATIVE (MN) WILLIAM FRENZEL,** September 18, 1990

Balancing the budget is like going to heaven. Everybody wants to do it, but nobody wants to do what you have to do to get there.

—**PHIL GRAMM,** *This Week With David Brinkley,* September 16, 1990

If we had a balanced budget amendment in the Constitution, in 10 years the Democratic Party could not and would not exist, because they are the party of government.

—**Senator Phil Gramm,** *Washington Post,* 1994

Balancing the budget is a fundamental condition of governing. For most of the nation's history, balancing budgets in peacetime was assumed as a normal operating procedure.

—**HENRY HYDE,** *USA Today,* January 26, 1995

There is a better way to bring down the deficit. Instead of raising taxes and discouraging saving, why not restrain government spending, eliminate unnecessary programs, and combine it with a tax policy which would create strong economic growth?

—**JACK KEMP,** *National Review,* March 21, 1994

The size of the federal budget is not an appropriate barometer of social conscience or charitable concern.

—**RONALD REAGAN,** October 5, 1981

We don't have a trillion-dollar debt because we haven't taxed enough; we have a trillion-dollar debt because we spend too much.

—**RONALD REAGAN,** March 28, 1982

Communism and the Cold War

It is said that each president will be recalled by posterity—with but a single sentence. George Washington was the father of our country. Abraham Lincoln preserved the Union. And Ronald Reagan won the Cold War.

—**PATRICK BUCHANAN,** August 17, 1992

What was wrong with communism wasn't aberrant leadership, it was communism.

—**WILLIAM F. BUCKLEY JR.,** *The Fresno Bee,* June 30, 1995

We face a hostile ideology—global in scope, atheistic in character, ruthless in purpose, and insidious in method.

—**DWIGHT D. EISENHOWER,** *from his farewell address to the nation,* January 17, 1961

Erect a "Victims of Communism Memorial" on the Mall. Whether Communism is headed for the ash heap of history or not, conservatives must never let the world forget the human cost of Communism—the tens of millions of innocents who died as a result of Communist tyranny. Communism's crimes against humanity cry out for an appropriate international memorial in the heart of Washington.

—**HENRY HYDE,** *Policy Review,* April 1990

The dominant school of American thought has it that a democratic, market-oriented Russia will reverse the nearly uninterrupted rhythm of four centuries of Russian expansionism.

Whether history will inevitably repeat itself is unanswerable.

Still, it is rare to find examples of 180-degree turns, if only because the geography never changes and because a shared historic memory is one of the most important components of the cohesion of any society.

I know no leader among Russia's neighboring countries—in or out of government—who shares America's faith in Russian conversion to Western modes of conduct.

—HENRY KISSINGER, *The Houston Chronicle,* April 25, 1993

Since the end of the Cold War, it has become apparent that fear of communism can no longer serve as the cement of the international order. With the collapse of the ideological challenge, traditional patterns of nationalism have gained ground nearly everywhere. The post-Cold War has already witnessed growing rivalries reminiscent of the tensions preceding World War I.

—HENRY KISSINGER, *Cleveland Plain Dealer,* July 18, 1993

It is the Soviet Union that runs against the tide of history. [It is] the march of freedom and democracy which will leave Marxism-Leninism on the ash heap of history as it has left other tyrannies which stifle the freedom and muzzle the self-expression of the people.

—RONALD REAGAN, *in a speech to Britain's Parliament,* 1982

The years ahead are great ones for this country, for the cause of freedom. . . . The West won't contain communism. It will transcend communism. It will dismiss it as some bizarre chapter in human history whose last pages are even now being written.

—RONALD REAGAN, *Notre Dame,* May 17, 1981

Let us beware that while they [Soviet rulers] preach the supremacy of the state, declare its omnipotence over individual man, and predict its eventual domination over all peoples of the earth, they are the focus of evil in the modern world. . . . I urge you to beware of the temptation . . . to ignore the facts of history and the aggressive impulses of any evil empire, to simply call the arms race a giant misunderstanding and thereby remove yourself from the struggle between right and wrong, good and evil.

—RONALD REAGAN, March 8, 1983

How do you tell a Communist? Well, it's someone who reads Marx and Lenin. And how do you tell an anti-Communist? It's someone who understands Marx and Lenin.

—RONALD REAGAN, September 25, 1987

The Economy

Know that euphemisms for restricting trade are created by those who benefit from restrictions.

—TEXAS REPRESENTATIVE DICK ARMEY, February 1993

Governments punish success and reward failure.

—DICK ARMEY, February 1993

Be skeptical of gloomy prognostications from people who are in the business of peddling more government.

—DICK ARMEY, February 1993

American economic history is a story of booms fading into resentment. It is not so much a business cycle as a cycle of public sentiment, alternating between times of optimism and times of pessimism. Between, if you must, decades of greed and, if you will, decades of envy.

—ROBERT L. BARTLEY, *The Seven Fat Years,* 1992

Young man, there is America which at this day serves for little more than to amuse you with stories of savage men and uncouth manners; yet shall, before you taste of death, show itself equal to the whole of that commerce which now attracts the envy of the world.

—**BRITISH STATESMAN EDMUND BURKE,** *Second Speech on Conciliation With America, The Thirteen Resolutions,* March 22, 1775

Since the late 1970s, market forces have fueled massive changes in the financial services industry. But the United States still relies on a regulatory system, born in the wake of the Great Depression, which stifles competition among providers of financial services.

—**ALFONSE D'AMATO,** *Roll Call,* March 27, 1995

This conjunction of an immense military establishment and a large arms industry is new in the American experience. We recognize the imperative need for this development. Yet we must not fail to comprehend its grave implications. In the councils of government, we must guard against the acquisition of unwarranted influence, whether sought or unsought, by the military-industrial complex. The potential for the disastrous rise of misplaced power exists and will persist.

—**DWIGHT D EISENHOWER,** *giving his farewell radio and television address to the American people,* January 17, 1961

What people have increasingly wanted government to do is: guarantee their jobs and incomes; protect them from foreign competition and limit the entry of new competitors at home; assure them "living wages" for their labor, and "fair" and "reasonable" prices for their products; protect them from the common mistakes of everyday life; and relieve them of any responsibility for the community efforts that would otherwise demand of them charity and the giving of some of their free time. And all these guarantees, protections, and securities are to be provided at someone else's expense. . . . The Age of Democratized Privilege has arrived. And with it has also come the New Protectionism.

—RICHARD M. EBELING, *Lecturing at Hillsdale College,* February, 1993

Capitalism works better than any of us can conceive. It is also the only truly moral system of exchange.

—MALCOLM FORBES JR., May 1993

Capitalism is the real enemy of tyranny.

—MALCOLM FORBES JR., May 1993

Japanese direct investment clearly increases job opportunities. Japanese financial investment does the same by making it possible to finance projects that could not otherwise have been financed. The dollars corresponding to the trade deficit do not disappear from the market; they are simply spent for something other than the items counted as exports of goods and services.

—**Milton Friedman,** *The Sacramento Bee,* August 12, 1993

The fiftieth anniversary of the Bretton Woods conference, which created the International Monetary Fund (IMF) and the International Bank for Reconstruction and Development (the World Bank), has been the occasion for a triumph of nostalgia over reality. Nostalgia has converted the twin institutions into major pillars of postwar expansion, transformed the 1971 termination of the system of pegged exchange rates established by Bretton Woods into a major policy mistake, and produced expressions of support for the re-establishment of such a system.

—**Milton Friedman,** *The National Review,* September 12, 1994

The political function of the income taxes, which is served by their being complex, is to provide a means whereby the members of Congress who have anything whatsoever to do with taxation can raise campaign funds. That is what supports the army of lobbyists in Washington who are seeking to produce changes in the income tax, to introduce special privileges or exemptions for their clients, or to have what they regard as special burdens on their clients removed.

—MILTON FRIEDMAN, *The San Francisco Examiner,* April 17, 1995

Most economic fallacies derive . . . from the tendency to assume that there is a fixed pie, that one party can gain only at the expense of another.

—MILTON FRIEDMAN, *Free to Choose,* (with Rose Friedman), 1980

The man has the gradually sinking feeling that his role as provider, the definitive male activity from the primal days of the hunt through the industrial revolution and on into modern life, has been largely seized from him; he has been cuckolded by the compassionate state.

—ECONOMIST GEORGE GILDER, *Wealth and Poverty,* 1993

Real poverty is less a state of income than a state of mind.

—GEORGE GILDER, *Wealth and Poverty,* 1993

A successful economy depends on the proliferation of the rich, on creating a large class of risk-taking men who are willing to shun the easy channels of a comfortable life in order to create new enterprise, win huge profits, and invest them again.

—GEORGE GILDER, *Wealth and Poverty,* 1993

Capitalism begins with giving. Not from greed, avarice, or even self love can one expect the rewards of commerce, but from a spirit closely akin to altruism, a regard for the needs of others, a benevolent, outgoing, and courageous temper of mind.

—GEORGE GILDER, *Wealth and Poverty,* 1993

I think that the record of Congress in being able to have a Keynesian micromanagement of the economy has been pretty pathetic, and I think you're much better off to establish a stable framework and then encourage entrepreneurs to go out and be productive and create new jobs. I think that's in the long run a much healthier system.

—NEWT GINGRICH, *I, Newt: The Quotations of Speaker Gingrich,* 1994

In all the world, only in North Korea, and in Cuba, and in the Democratic Party in Washington, D.C. today do we still have those in power who still believe that more government planning, more taxing, and more spending form the path for prosperity and opportunity.

—PHIL GRAMM, *at the New Hampshire Republican Convention,* January 31, 1993

Our position on prosperity is and has always been, and it has been distinct from the Democrats' position, that prosperity comes from giving people opportunity, that prosperity comes from free enterprise and limited government.

—**PHIL GRAMM,** *at the New Hampshire Republican Convention,* January 31, 1993

Diets and deficit reduction plans have one thing in common: It's not the ones that don't work that people quit. It's the ones that work all too well that we drop. They're just too tough. And when the Gramm-Rudman deficit reduction law was abandoned, the process resembled the way effective diets are forsaken.

—**PHIL GRAMM,** *The Washington Times,* June 25, 1993

Nobody riding in the wagon should be any better off than someone pulling the wagon. A person qualifying for four major welfare programs receives $21,000 annually, compared with $8,800 for someone earning minimum wage.

—**PHIL GRAMM,** *The Washington Times,* January 4, 1995

The frightening but inescapable conclusion of any honest look at where we are as a nation has got to lead us to believe we're either going to change the way we do business or we are going to lose the American dream.

—**PHIL GRAMM,** *The Washington Post,* February 25, 1995

Eliminating the capital gains tax would dramatically expand entrepreneurship and job creation in our nation's most distressed communities. Existing incentives in Clinton's plan are useful if you already own a business with significant payroll, but the capital gains tax, primarily a penalty on risk-taking, is the major obstacle facing the creation of new businesses.

—JACK KEMP, June 18, 1993

Today, the greatest obstacle facing the poor inner cities and rural communities is the federal government. High taxes on capital formation and heavy government regulation are draining any hope for investment, entrepreneurship, and job creation out of America's inner cities.

—JACK KEMP, June 18, 1993

It is time to reverse America's noncompetitiveness in savings, investments and long-term holdings.

—MICHAEL NOVAK, Political Commentator and Co-host of Evans & Novak, Forbes, September 4, 1989

Capitalism is . . . a social order favorable to alertness, inventiveness, discovery, and creativity. This means a social order based upon education, research, the freedom to create, and the right to enjoy the fruit's of one's own creativity.

—MICHAEL NOVAK, *Errand Into the Wilderness,* 1956

If you ask me to name the proudest distinction of Americans, I would choose—because it contains all the others—the fact that they were the people who created the phrase "to make money." No other language nation has ever used these words before; men had always thought of wealth as a static quality—to be seized, begged, inherited, shared, looted, or obtained as a favor. Americans were the first to understand that wealth has to be created.

—PHILOSOPHER AND AUTHOR AYN RAND, *Atlas Shrugged,* 1957

Leave all creative energies uninhibited. Merely organize society to act in harmony with this lesson. Let society's legal apparatus remove all obstacles the best it can. Permit creative know-how to freely flow. Have faith that free men will respond to the "Invisible Hand" [Adam Smith's invisible hand at work in the free market].

—LEONARD E. READ, 1958

We who live in free Market societies believe that growth, prosperity and ultimately human fulfillment, are created from the bottom up, not the government down. Only when the human spirit is allowed to invent and create, only when individuals are given a personal stake in deciding economic policies and benefiting from their success—only then can societies remain economically alive, dynamic, progressive, and free. Trust the people. This is one irrefutable lesson of the entire postwar period contradicting the notion that rigid government controls are essential to economic development.

—RONALD REAGAN, September 29, 1981

While economic growth may not be a sufficient condition for keeping deficits down, it is nevertheless an absolutely necessary condition. Just imagine the budget consequences of another recession or a slow-growth economy.

—VIN WEBER, *The Washington Times,* June 23, 1995

Conservatives and free market principles dictate that political leaders today should want a highly competitive national telephone system, unfettered by regulation, and able to slug it out in the marketplace for paying customers. . . . That's why conservatives in America today support legislation that would make the local telephone markets—now dominated by seven Bell monopolies— become just as competitive as their long distance brethren.

—VIN WEBER, *The Washington Times,* May 7, 1995

Education

We must develop a fair appreciation for the real strengths and limitations of government effort on behalf of children. Government, obviously, cannot fill a child's emotional needs. Nor can it fill his spiritual and moral needs. Government is not a father or mother. Government has never raised a child, and it never will.

—WILLIAM J. BENNETT, October 1990

If my own son, who is now 10 months, came to me and said, "You promised to pay for my tuition at Harvard: how about giving me $50,000 instead to start a little business?" I might think that was a good idea.

—WILLIAM J. BENNETT, *The New York Times,* February 12, 1985

Our common language is . . . English. And our common task is to ensure that our non-English speaking children learn this common language.

—WILLIAM J. BENNETT, *The New York Times,* September 26, 1985

The elementary school must assume as its sublime and most solemn responsibility the task of teaching every child in it to read. Any school that does not acccomplish this has failed.

—WILLIAM J. BENNETT, *The New York Times,* September 3, 1986

[E]ducation is, after all, a serious business. Its lifeblood is standards. If there are no standards, how do we call something higher education?

—WILLIAM J. BENNETT, *address at the University of Notre Dame,* October 1990

The secretary of education does not work for the education establishment. The secretary works for the American people.

—WILLIAM J. BENNETT, *Christian Science Monitor,* March 12, 1985

I do not suggest that you should not have an open mind, particularly as you approach college. But, don't keep your mind so open that your brains fall out.

—WILLIAM J. BENNETT, *address to Gonzaga College High School,* 1987

Most education certification today is pure "credentialism." [It] must begin to reflect our demand for excellence, not our appreciation of parchment.

—WILLIAM J. BENNETT, *The New York Times,* September 3, 1986

Remember: the child is not a ward given to the state for its nurture. The child is a gift of God given in trust to his parents. Schools should treat young people as gifts of God, not as subjects of social experimentation.

—**WILLIAM J. BENNETT,** *address to Republican Convention Speech,* August 19, 1992

[The shortage of student loans] may require . . . divestiture of certain sorts—stereo divestiture, automobile divestiture, three-weeks-at-the-beach divestiture.

—WILLIAM J. BENNETT, *The New York Times,* February 12, 1985

American public education is organized exactly like Soviet agriculture was organized. It is a bureaucratic, top-heavy system with every decision directed from above.

—PETER M. FLANIGAN, *Imprimis,* June, 1993

Education is the largest socialist institution in the United States today. As such, it performs like all socialist institutions. It produces a very inefficient product at high cost and benefits a favored few. And there is no way to change it except by competition and choice.

—MILTON FRIEDMAN, *The San Francisco Chronicle,* October 11, 1993

[To believe that] no one was ever corrupted by a book, you almost have to believe that no one was ever improved by a book (or play, or a movie). . . . No one, not even a university professor, really believes that.

—EDITOR AND AUTHOR IRVING KRISTOL, *Reflections of a Neo-Conservative,* 1993

A friend was startled recently by hearing his teenage daughter express at the dinner table her fears about the future: "And" she added to a long list, "the ozone layer is being destroyed by industry, and there won't be any world left by the time our generation has grandchildren." He demurred weakly and she rushed on: "We just studied it in school!"

All over the country, it seems, our educational system is scaring our children half to death, poisoning their confidence and destroying their hope in this nation's future.

—MICHAEL NOVAK, *Political Commentator and co-host of Evans & Novak,* *Forbes,* October 30, 1989

The things that happened in academia in the 1960s, 1970s and 1980s led to dangerous politicization that is inimicable to what colleges and universities should be doing . . . this is an attack on the very idea of meritocracy, objectivity and neutral principles. . . . There is much more pressure to conform on campus that in the larger society.

—JAMES PIERSON, *The Boston Globe,* November 12, 1990

There are no such things as limits to growth, because there are no limits on the human capacity for intelligence, imagination and wonder.

—RONALD REAGAN, *address at the University of South Carolina, Columbia,* September 20, 1983

———————

Many teachers now consider the traditional idea of teaching to be intellectually suspect and morally offensive because it is tainted by the authoritarian idea that there are defensible standards and by the inegalitarian idea that some people do things better than others. The idea of transmitting skills and standards was inherently threatening to the values of that decade—spontaneity, authenticity, sincerity, equality and self-esteem. Education in the new era of enlightenment was to be a matter of putting things into students but of letting things out.

—GEORGE WILL, *The Dallas Morning News,* July 9, 1995

Foreign Policy

Thanks to Aldrich Ames, it may be another generation before a freedom-loving North Korean, Chinese, Iraqi, Iranian or Libyan takes the risk of sending secrets for the benefit of the United

States. But that we must make the effort to penetrate to the secret designs and resources of such countries would appear to be a strategy more important, even, than an auto-da-fé over our mishandling of the traitor Ames.

—WILLIAM F. BUCKLEY JR., *The Cincinnati Enquirer,* July 6, 1995

Much good can come from the prudent use of power.

—GEORGE BUSH, *1992 State of the Union Speech*

A President's most important commodity as Commander-in-Chief is his credibility. Bold talk that is never followed up by bold action leads our adversaries to conclude we do not have to be taken seriously. The cost of reclaiming that credibility once it is lost is likely to be paid in terms of American lives. In these dangerous times, a President must always say what he means and mean what he says.

—SECRETARY OF DEFENSE DICK CHENEY, July 27, 1994

It is not given to us to peer into the mysteries of the future. Still, I avow my hope and faith, sure and inviolate, that in the days to come the British and American peoples will for their own safety and for the good of all walk together side by side in majesty, in justice, and in peace.

—WINSTON CHURCHILL, December 26, 1941

An appeaser is one who feeds a crocodile—hoping it will eat him last.

—**WINSTON CHURCHILL,** *Reader's Digest,* December 1954

I have long held that the current Arab-Israeli peace process must be judged by one question, and one question only: Will Israel be stronger and more secure at the end of the process than it was at the beginning?

To help achieve that end, I strongly advocate moving the US Embassy to Jerusalem and recognizing Israel's sovereignty over an undivided Jerusalem.

—**PHIL GRAMM,** *The Jerusalem Post,* April 7, 1995

Democracy is no panacea for all the world's ills. But democrats have proven themselves far more likely to pursue nonviolent means of redressing longstanding ethnic and national grievances than their authoritarian or totalitarian counterparts. Moreover, there is something distasteful about the United States—the world's premier multiracial, multiethnic, religiously plural democracy—showing sympathy for the difficulties of Chinese tyrants or Soviet reform communists. A democratic revolution has been sweeping across that globe for the past decade. We should not resist the winds of freedom in the name of a misconstrued "prudence" or, worse, an amoral Realpolitik. Rather, we should try to help direct the democratic revolution so that is produces what it promises: governments accountable to the consent of the governed.

—**HENRY HYDE,** *Chicago Tribune,* September 9, 1991

In matters of national security, the balance between Congress and the president should always tilt significantly toward the chief executive. But when an administration so woefully weakens our nation's hand internationally, thus endangering our national security, Congress must assert itself. Legislating severe limitations on a president's foreign policy is rarely appropriate. It must be contemplated only as a last resort. But until this administration places the interests of the American people above all else—including "multilateralism"—ruling out a legislative response would be just as irresponsible.

—**HENRY HYDE,** *The Washington Post,* October 26, 1993

Treaties have to be taken as seriously as constitutional amendments. Once ratified, they cannot easily be renounced.

—**COLUMINIST JAMES KILPATRICK,** *St. Petersburg Times,* May 18, 1991

International systems live precariously. Every "world order" exprcsscs an aspiration to permanence; yet the elements that make up a world order are in constant flux and the duration of international systems has been shrinking.

—**HENRY KISSINGER,** *Time,* March 14, 1994

Once again, American policy toward Russia is being presented largely in terms of supporting a particular Russian leader. First it was Mikhail Gorbachev; now it is Boris Yeltsin. Failure to extend him aid, it is said, will bring into power sinister Communist holdouts and Cold War policies that will cost us more than any conceivable aid program.

—**HENRY KISSINGER,** *The Washington Post,* March 23, 1993

The two great challenges of the contemporary period—the integration of a united Germany into the West and the acceptance by Russia of her national frontiers—reqiure a close North Atlantic relationship that, in contrast to the Cold War period, emphasizes political goals.

—**HENRY KISSINGER,** *The Los Angeles Times,* April 25, 1993

America can neither give a veto over the defense of its interests to international institutions nor permit multilateralism to invoke American forces where no significant national interests are involved.

—**HENRY KISSINGER,** *The Washington Post,* September 8, 1993

Avoiding disaster cannot remain the sole test of American foreign policy.

—HENRY KISSINGER, *The Houston Chronicle,* February 27, 1994

America and China have a parallel interest in equilibrium in Asia.

—HENRY KISSINGER, *The Washington Post,* March 28, 1994

By far the most worrisome aspect of American foreign policy—far more troubling than Bosnia and Haiti—is the progressive erosion of the Atlantic Alliance, for half a century the keystone of American diplomacy. It goes without saying that the disintegration of the Soviet empire, the retreat of Soviet armies and the unification of Germany require major changes in NATO structure and purpose. What is taking place is not adaptation, however, so much as decline into an empty shell and with nary a public discussion.

—HENRY KISSINGER, *The Washington Post,* August 16, 1994

The statesman's duty is to bridge the gap between his nations experience and his vision.

—HENRY KISSINGER, *Years of Upheaval,* 1982

Peacemaking by the United Nations spells war. And when Americans get killed, the administration in office must be able to explain what American interests and values are involved. Moreover, military operations presuppose a military strategy and command system, both tasks for which the U.N. machinery has proven supremely unsuited.

—HENRY KISSINGER, *The Washington Post,* March 9, 1995

The American temptation is to believe that foreign policy is a subdivision of psychiatry.

—HENRY KISSINGER, *Time,* June 17, 1985

In crises the most daring course is often safest.

—HENRY KISSINGER, *Years of Upheaval,* 1982

No foreign policy—no matter how ingenious—has any chance of success if it is borne on the minds of a few and carried in the hearts of none.

—HENRY KISSINGER, *speaking to International Platform Association,*
August 2, 1973

Because of the pervasive bugging, I did not dictate any diary entries while we were in the Soviet Union. The Soviets were curiously unsubtle in this regard. A member of my staff reported having casually told his secretary that he would like an apple, and 10 minutes later a maid came and put a bowl of apples on the table.

—RICHARD M. NIXON, *talking about his visit to the Soviet Union in May 1972, Memoirs, 1978*

I certainly agree that we should not go around saying we are the world's policemen. But guess who gets called when someone needs a cop?

—COLIN POWELL, *New York Times, August 17, 1990*

Perestroika is nothing more than refined Stalinism.

—DAN QUAYLE, *September 4, 1988*

I just don't think it's good for us to be run out of town.

—RONALD REAGAN, *refusing to cancel Secretary of State Schultz's trip to Moscow after the discovery of listening devices in the U.S. embassy there, Time, April 20, 1987*

Isn't it strange that people build walls to keep an enemy out, and there's only one philosophy where they have to build walls to keep their people in?

—**RONALD REAGAN,** *commenting on the Berlin Wall,* August 12, 1986

One difference between French appeasement and American appeasement is that France pays ransom in cash and gets its hostages back while the United States pays ransom in arms and gets additional hostages taken.

—**COLUMNIST WILLIAM SAFIRE,** *The New York Times,* November 13, 1986

Ninety-nine years have passed since Theodor Herzl, appalled by anti-Semitism during the 1894 Dreyfus trial, energized the Zionist movement that produced the Jewish state. Now, it suddenly seems probable that there soon will be a second Palestinian state, of sorts.

What sort? On the answer to that question, the survival of the Jewish state depends.

Israel is attempting to trade land for peace. The trouble with such trades is this asymmetry: Israel yields something tangible and gets only promises that might prove as evanescent as Hitler's promise, after Munich, that he had made his last territorial demand.

—**GEORGE WILL,** *Chicago Sun-Times,* September 9, 1993

Taxes: Even Einstein Couldn't Understand His 1040 Form

In the old days, when free Americans paid their taxes out of their own wallets, there was a limit to how much revenue our statists could raise without having a rebellion on their hands. People could see how much they paid the government, and judge if the return was worth it. But once World War II gave the statists an excuse to take our money from our paychecks before we even touched it, the obscene growth of the government became inexorable.

—DICK ARMEY, *Policy Review*, July 1994

For Washington to put at the disposal of the states its elaborate machinery of tax collection is to hoodwink apparent accountability. It leaves the states in a position comparable to the heir whose only responsibility is to decide how to allocate the money he has just now inherited.

—WILLIAM F. BUCKLEY JR., *The Buffalo News*, April 10, 1995

To tax and to please, no more that to love and to be wise, is not given to man.

—EDMUND BURKE, *in a speech at his arrival at Bristol*, October 13, 1774

The Congress will push me to raise taxes, and I'll say no, and they'll push and I'll say no, and they'll push again, and I'll say to them, "Read my lips: no new taxes."

—**GEORGE BUSH,** *1992 Republican Convention*

Inflaton is taxation without legislation.

—**MILTON FRIEDMAN,** 1979

If your taxes were lower because of a Republican majority in Congress, what would you spend the extra money on? Your children? Their college education? Put it in savings? Make some investments? Pay off some bills?

—**NEWT GINGRICH,** *I Newt: The Quotations of Speaker Gingrich,* 1994

I want to take on an issue that so few in our ranks are willing to take on: taxing the rich. You know, there is only one form of bigotry that is acceptable in America, and that is bigotry against the people who work and save and succeed. It is an absolute outrage. Today, the top one percent of income earners pay 40% more of the overall income tax burden in this country than they did when Ronald Reagan became President of the United States. The collection of taxes has become more progressive, not less progressive. Even though we have lowered the rates, we have done away with deductions, and we have made the tax system more efficient. But, if you believe you can raise taxes by 30% on people who have succeeded and not have the economy feel it, you are absolutely wrong. People get rich in America by being successful, by investing and creating jobs, growth and opportunity.

—PHIL GRAMM, *from his speech at the Conservative Political Action Conference in Washington, D.C.,* February 18, 1993

Taxes carry economic costs wholly apart from their expense to taxpayers. A tax on theater tickets would hurt attendance, for instance, and an income-tax rise would dampen citizen's incentive to do productive work. Although comon sense says Government should minimize these costs, the [Clinton] Administration is unfortunately relying more and more on one of the most economically expensive of all taxes: levies on stock.

—PHIL GRAMM, *The New York Times,* May 22, 1994

Taxing the rich and foreign corporations won't give President Clinton the revenue he needs. To make up the difference, he'll have to go after "loopholes" and enforcement, and he'll have to raise taxes further down the income ladder. These and other tax increases will slow economic growth, restrain the rise in federal revenue, and play havoc with the deficit.

—JAMES C. MILLER III, *Policy Review,* January 1993

The current tax code is a daily mugging.

—RONALD REAGAN, September 2, 1985

Most tax revisions didn't improve the system, they made it more like Washington itself; complicated, unfair, cluttered with gobbledygook and loopholes designed for those with the power and influence to hire high-priced legal and tax advisers.

—RONALD REAGAN, *address to the nation,* May 28, 1985

Even Albert Einstein reportedly needed help on his 1040 form.

—RONALD REAGAN, *address to the nation,* May 28, 1985

Fiscal problems do a lot for moral uplift because sin takes a terrific shellacking from sin taxes.

—GEORGE WILL, *The Washington Post,* February 26, 1989

LAW AND ORDER

The Scales of Justice

Law is vulnerable to the winds of intellectual or moral fashion, which it then validates as the commands of our most basic concept.

—ROBERT H. BORK, *The New York Times*, January 4, 1985

Our sworn duty to "ensure domestic Tranquility" is as old as the Republic, placed in the Constitution's preamble even before the common defense and the general welfare. When we ask what kind of society the American people deserve, our goal must be a Nation in which law-abiding citizens are safe and feel safe.

—GEORGE BUSH, May 1989

They say that as long as he can afford top-flight counsel, Mr. [O.J.] Simpson eventually could well go free whether or not he committed the crime.

This suggestion—hire 10 top-flight lawyers and go free—dismays a society concerned with effective justice. It surely appalls the families of Nicole Brown Simpson and Ronald Goldman. And it reminds us forcefully that the justice system is terribly awry.

—**WILLIAM F. BUCKLEY JR.**, *The Buffalo News*, April 15, 1995

We as a society need to re-examine our deluded ideas about crime and punishment. For at least thirty years, "root causes" for crimes have become our obsession. Those "root causes" are still with us while America's crime rates have tripled.

—**JAY DICKEY, ARKANSAS REPRESENTATIVE,** July 1994

Crazy loopholes and arcane technicalities that free violent criminals to roam the streets—placing their rights ahead of their victims'—will be ended under Republican leadership.

—**NEWT GINGRICH,** *I, Newt: The Quotations of the Speaker Gingrich*, 1994

Contrary to conventional wisdom, most criminals are perfectly rational men and women. They don't commit crimes because they're in the grip of some irresistible impulse. They commit crimes because they think it pays. Unfortunately, in most cases they are right: In America today, crime does pay.

—**PHIL GRAMM,** *The New York Times*, July 8, 1993

Until those of us who aren't victims of crime are as outraged as those who are, crime in America will continue to grow.

—**PHIL GRAMM,** *The Houston Chronicle*, November 2, 1993

Keeping these irredeemable predators in prison for life—or at least for as many years as it takes to drain the criminality out of them—is the single most effective step we can take to combat repeated violent crime. Not only will they be removed from their customary prey, but their tough sentences will deter others from following in their footsteps.

—**HENRY HYDE,** *The Washington Times*, April 3, 1994

Many liberals resist the notion of building more prisons because they feel a disproportionate number of minorities will be imprisoned. This concern for minorities, while admirable, leads to disastrous consequences for the minority community as a whole because it is that community, more than any other, that is being savaged by crime in present-day America. And it is the minority community that would most benefit from a diminution of crime.

—**HENRY HYDE,** *Roll Call*, August 8, 1994

From time to time, we iconoclasts in the press gallery complain that the nine Supremes aren't doing enough work to justify their $164,000 salaries. Each of them should be writing at least a dozen opinions for the court every term, but in this past term Justices Scalia, Thomas, Souter and Breyer wrote only eight apiece, and Justices O'Connor and Ginsburg wrote only nine. This is not what you would call heavy lifting.

—COLUMNIST JAMES KILPATRICK, *The Buffalo News*, July 8, 1995

I have spent nearly 50 years as a reporter covering "the law." I am wearily aware that if an arrest ever is made, the probabilities are strong that the accused will slip through holes in the net. The warrant will be defective, or the Miranda rights will not have been properly read, or a jury will not have been correctly impaneled. I believe deeply in constitutional rights and the rule of law, but disillusion seeps in. I am sick of societal attitudes that coddle the venomous spider and disdain the innocent fly.

—JAMES KILPATRICK, *The Courier-Journal*, April 18, 1989

The idea that police cannot ask questions of the person that knows most about the crime is an infamous decision.

—EDWIN MEESE 3RD, *The New York Times*, September 1, 1985

The imperial Congress clearly likes having its own imperial prosecutor. The independent counsel statute, passed by Congress in 1978, is a loaded gun that Congress gets to hold to the president's head. With a presidential election coming up next

Our chief justices have probably had more profound and lasting influence in their times and on the direction of the nation than most presidents.

—RICHARD M. NIXON, *on the appointment of Warren E. Burger as Chief Justice,* May 21, 1969

year, Walsh is just beginning to squeeze the trigger. That's why, when they wrote the law creating this constitutional anomaly, Congress decided that special prosecutors would investigate people, rather than crimes. That way, they can pick through every facet of an executive branch official's life until they discover a crime to hang him with. Mao Tse-tung employed this technique as part of his so-called cultural revolution. Stalin had another term. He called it a purge.

—**OLIVER NORTH,** *St. Louis Post-Dispatch*, July 12, 1991

The criminal element now calculates that crime really does pay.

—**RONALD REAGAN,** April 18, 1984

Government has an important role to play to restore law and justice but federal programs cannot rebuild a shattered moral order, a self-indulgent popular culture, educational failure and the breakdown of church and family. We must affirm our belief and conviction in individual responsibility, civic duty, and obedience to the law. We will not accomplish these goals with another Great Society bill out of Washington, DC.

—**PAT ROBERTS,** *Kansas Representative,* September 1994

The Freedom of Information Act is the Taj Mahal of the Doctrine of Unanticipated Consequences, the Sistine Chapel of Cost-Benefit Analysis Ignored.

—**ANTONIN SCALIA,** *Supreme Court Justice, Time*, June 30, 1986

Convicted murderers should not be allowed to take advantage of an already clogged court system to get bogged down in an endless argument over statistics.

—**FRED THOMPSON,** *as a candidate for the U.S. Senate, The Commercial Appeal*, April 26, 1994

Increasingly in many urban areas civil society no longer exists. The streets are ruled by gangs, drug dealers, and hired gunmen. The areas controlled by criminal elements are expanding, not shrinking. It will not be long before suburbanites are directly affected, as some already have been by crimes like carjacking. When that happens, we will be poised to cross the line from criminal activity into internal war. Successive governments have labelled this problem "too hard" and swept it under the rug. It only gets harder with time; we have to deal with it now, before we have a war on our hands.

—**PAUL M. WEYRICH,** *Policy Review*, January 1993

The Constitution and the Law

The less people know about how sausages and laws are made, the better they'll sleep at night.

—OTTO VON BISMARCK, *Attributed*

The American legal system is systematically skewed in favor of plaintiffs on the assumption that there is a limitless number of serious injustices so that making plaintiffs' victories ever easier is a pure social good. To accomplish that, pleading requirements have been relaxed so that a defendant often finds it impossible to know exactly what he is alleged to have done wrong, or to be sure that the nature of the charge against him won't change several times during the proceedings to fit the plaintiff's tactical convenience.

—ROBERT H. BORK, *The Washington Times*, April 29, 1991

The First Amendment is about how we govern ourselves—not about how we titillate ourselves sexually.

—ROBERT H. BORK, ABC's *This Week with David Brinkley*, June 25, 1989

The judge's authority derives entirely from the fact that he is to apply the law and not his personal values. That is why the American public accepts the decisions of its courts, accepts even decisions that nullify the laws a majority of the electorate or their representatives voted for.

—**ROBERT H. BORK**, 1987

The conventional wisdom, echoed on almost all editorial pages, holds that an independent counsel is essential because the Department of Justice cannot be trusted to prosecute miscreants in the executive branch. The conventional wisdom is wrong. The main problem is that the independent counsel is accountable to no one.

—**ROBERT H. BORK**, *Commentary*, February 1993

When a judge applies a statute, he asks: "What did Congress understand itself to be doing with this statute?" Since the Constitution is a legal document, it should be approached in the same way. The danger comes when the Court cuts loose from that standard method of interpretation and begins to act as the final legislature, allowing justices to write their own moral or political principles into the Constitution. Because then we've essentially lost our form of government.

—**ROBERT H. BORK**, *Life*, Fall 1991

The meaning of the Constitution of the United States, it turns out, is no more and no less than one's heart's desire. Both constitutional jurisprudence and constitutional scholarship are largely exercises in wish fulfillment. That conservative intellectuals are as guilty of this as Liberal intellectuals probably means that a jurisprudence of the actual principles of the Constitution as those were understood by the men who made them law is impossible for the foreseeable future.

—ROBERT H. BORK, *National Review*, February 7, 1994

The First Amendment's establishment clause—"Congress shall make no law respecting an establishment of religion"—clearly precludes recognition of an official church, and it can easily be read to prevent discriminatory aid to one or a few religions. But it hardly requires the conclusion that government may not assist religion in general or sponsor religious symbolism. An established religion is one which the state recognizes as the official religion and which it organizes by law. Typically, citizens are required to support the established church by taxation. The Congress that proposed and the states that ratified the First Amendment knew very well what an establishment of religion was, since six states had various forms of establishment at the time; ironically, one reason for the prohibition was to save these state establishments from federal interference.

—ROBERT H. BORK, *Commentary*, February, 1995

Those who made and endorsed our Constitution knew man's nature, and it is to their ideas, rather than to the temptations of utopia, that we must ask that our judges adhere.

—ROBERT H. BORK, *The Tempting of America*, 1989

When a judge goes beyond [his proper function] and reads entirely new values into the Constitution, values the framers and ratifiers did not put there, he deprives the people of their liberty. That liberty, which the Constitution clearly envisions, is the liberty of the people to set their own social agenda through the process of democracy.

—ROBERT H. BORK, 1987

It is not, what a lawyer tells me I may do; but what humanity, reason, and justice, tell me I ought to do.

—EDMUND BURKE, *Second Speech on Conciliation With America: The Thirteen Resolutions*, March 22, 1775

[P]ersonal freedom is best maintained . . . when it is ingrained in a people's habits and not enforced against popular policy by the coercion of adjudicated law.

—SUPREME COURT JUSTICE FELIX FRANKFURTER, 1939

It is of the essence of the demand for equality before the law that people should be treated alike in spite of the fact that they are different.

—ECONOMIST FREDRICH HAYEK, *The Constitution of Liberty*, 1960

The great aim of the struggle for liberty has been equality before the law.

—FRIEDRICH HAYEK, *The Constitution of Liberty*, 1960

Federal and state officials now have the power to seize your business, home, bank account, records and personal property—all without indictment, hearing or trial. Everything you have can be taken away at the whim of one or two federal or state officials. Regardless of sex, age, race or economic situation, we are all potential victims.

Just ask Willie Jones, owner of a Nashville landscaping business. In 1991, he made the mistake of paying for an airplane ticket in cash—behavior deemed to fit a drug courier profile. Jones was detained and his luggage searched. No drugs were found. But in his wallet was $9,600 in cash. The money was seized, but Jones was not charged with any crime. After two years of legal wrangling, Jones' money was returned.

Increased government and police powers, rising criminal activity and violence, popular anxiety about drug use—all have become justifications for curtailing the application of the Bill of Rights and the individual security it once guaranteed.

Reform is long overdue.

—**HENRY HYDE,** *USA Today*, July 11, 1995

My view is that judicial power is legitimate only if the Constitution is law, which means that the judge applies principles that are both independent of his or her desires and that those principles have been adopted by the political community in one of the ways we recognize as a way of making law. This is the view called originalism, and it is despised by those who want judges to produce results the ratifiers never intended and modern legislatures will not vote.

—**SUPREME COURT JUSTICE CLARENCE THOMAS,** *Chicago Tribune*, December 9, 1987

A CONSERVATIVE PHILOSOPHY OF LIFE

Pearls of Wisdom

The real community of man, in the midst of all the self-contradictory simulacra of community, is the community of those who seek the truth.

—**ALLAN BLOOM,** *The Closing of the American Mind*, 1987

The concessions of the weak are the concessions of fear.

—**EDMUND BURKE,** *Second Speech on Conciliation With America: The Thirteen Resolutions*, March 22, 1775

There is, however, a limit at which forbearance ceases to be a virtue.

—**EDMUND BURKE,** *Observations on a Late Publication on the Present State of the Nation*, 1769

I mean to live my life an obedient man, but obedient to God, subservient to the wisdom of my ancestors; never to the authority of political truths arrived at yesterday at the voting booth.

—WILLIAM F. BUCKLEY JR., *Up From Liberalism,* 1959

People will not look forward to posterity who never look backward to their ancestors.

—**EDMUND BURKE,** *Reflections on the Revolution in France*, 1790

The only thing necessary for the triumph of evil is for good men to do nothing.

—**EDMUND BURKE,** *Attributed*

A fanatic is one who can't change his mind and won't change the subject.

—**WINSTON CHURCHILL,** July 5, 1954

Humility must always be the portion of any man who receives acclaim earned in the blood of his followers and the sacrifices of his friends.

—**DWIGHT D. EISENHOWER,** July 12, 1945

What counts is not necessarily the size of the dog in the fight— it's the size of the fight in the dog.

—**DWIGHT D. EISENHOWER,** 1958

Courage is contagious. When a brave man takes a stand, the spines of others are often stiffened.

—**BILLY GRAHAM,** *Reader's Digest*, July 1964

Those who say life is worth living at any cost have already written for themselves an epitaph of infamy, for there is no cause and no person they will not betray to stay alive.

—SOCIAL PHILOSOPHER SIDNEY HOOK, *Attributed*

There are no limits on our future if we don't put limits on our people.

—JACK KEMP, April 6, 1987

Not by force of arms are civilizations held together, but by subtle threads of moral and intellectual principle.

—JOURNALIST RUSSELL KIRK, *Enlivening the Conservative Mind,* 1953

Privilege, in any society, is the reward of duties performed.

—RUSSELL KIRK, *Enlivening the Conservative Mind,* 1953

Truth, which is most important to a scholar, has got to be concrete. And there is nothing more concrete than dealing with babies, burps and bottles, frogs and mud.

—JEANE H. KIRKPATRICK, *Newsweek*, January 3, 1983

We must learn to distinguish morality from moralizing.

—HENRY KISSINGER, 1976

History knows no resting places and no plateaus.

—HENRY KISSINGER, *White House Years*, 1979

You've got to learn to survive a defeat. That's when you develop character.

—RICHARD M. NIXON, *Dallas Times-Herald*, December 10, 1978

A man is not finished when he is defeated. He is finished when he quits.

—RICHARD M. NIXON, *Dallas Times-Herald*, December 10, 1978

In the end what matters is that you have always lived life to the hilt. I have won some great victories and suffered some devastating defeats. But win or lose, I feel fortunate to have come to that time in life when I can finally enjoy what my Quaker grandmother would have called "peace at the center."

—RICHARD M. NIXON, *In the Arena*, 1990

A CONSERVATIVE PHILOSOPHY OF LIFE

There is only one basic human right, the right to do what you damn well please.

—**P. J. O'ROURKE,** *1993 Speech to the Cato Institute*

To sit back hoping that someday, some way, someone will make things right is to go on feeding the crocodile, hoping he will eat you last—but eat you he will.

—**RONALD REAGAN,** November 7, 1974

Why do you climb philosophical hills? Because they are worth climbing. . . . There are no hills to go own unless you start from the top.

—**MARGARET THATCHER,** *remarks to Israeli Institute for Advanced Political and Strategic Studies, Wall Street Journal,* August 8, 1986

Pessimism is as American as apple pie—frozen apple pie with a slice of processed cheese.

—**GEORGE WILL,** *Statecraft as Soulcraft,* 1983

There may be more poetry than justice in poetic justice.

—**GEORGE WILL,** *The Pursuit of Virtue and Other Tory Notions,* 1982